Lee Spinks

Routledge
Taylor & Francis Group

LONDON AND NEW YORK

First published 2003
by Routledge
2 Park Square, Milton Park, Abingdon, Oxon OX14 4RN

Simultaneously published in the USA and Canada
by Routledge
270 Madison Avenue, New York, NY 10016

Routledge is an imprint of the Taylor & Francis Group

© 2003 Lee Spinks

Typeset in Perpetua by
Florence Production Ltd, Stoodleigh, Devon

British Library Cataloguing in Publication Data
A catalogue record for this book is available from the British Library.

Library of Congress Cataloging in Publication Data
Spinks, Lee, 1963–
  Friedrich Nietzsche / Lee Spinks.
    p. cm. – (Routledge critical thinkers)
  Includes bibliographical references and index.
  1. Nietzsche, Friedrich Wilhelm, 1844–1900. I. Title. II. Series.
  B3317.S64 2003
  193–dc21   2002151163

ISBN 0–415–26360–3 (pbk)
ISBN 0–415–26359–X (hbk)

FRIEDRICH NIETZSCHE

It is difficult to imagine a world without common sense, the distinction between truth and falsehood, the belief in some form of morality or an agreement that we are all human. But Friedrich Nietzsche did imagine such a world, and his work has become a crucial point of departure for contemporary critical theory and debate. This volume offers a lucid and accessible account of Nietzsche's philosophy, encompassing such ideas as anti-humanism, good and evil, nihilism and the will to power, and introduces the reader to the radical questions posed by Nietzsche that challenged the received history of thought. The author not only prepares readers for their first encounter with Nietzsche's most influential texts, but enables them to begin to apply his philosophy in studies of literature, art and contemporary culture.

Lee Spinks is a lecturer in English Literature at the University of Edinburgh. He has published articles on literary theory, modern and postmodern culture and contemporary American literature.

ROUTLEDGE CRITICAL THINKERS
essential guides for literary studies

Series Editor: Robert Eaglestone, Royal Holloway, University of London

Routledge Critical Thinkers is a series of accessible introductions to key figures in contemporary critical thought.

With a unique focus on historical and intellectual contexts, each volume examines a key theorist's:

- significance
- motivation
- key ideas and their sources
- impact on other thinkers

Concluding with extensively annotated guides to further reading, *Routledge Critical Thinkers* are the literature student's passport to today's most exciting critical thought.

Already available:
Jean Baudrillard by Richard J. Lane
Maurice Blanchot by Ullrich Haase and William Large
Judith Butler by Sara Salih
Gilles Deleuze by Claire Colebrook
Sigmund Freud by Pamela Thurschwell
Martin Heidegger by Timothy Clark
Fredric Jameson by Adam Roberts
Jean-François Lyotard by Simon Malpas
Paul de Man by Martin McQuillan
Paul Ricoeur by Karl Simms
Edward Said by Bill Ashcroft and Pal Ahluwalia
Gayatri Chakravorty Spivak by Stephen Morton

For further details on this series, see www.literature.routledge.com/rct

CONTENTS

CONTENTS

SERIES EDITOR'S PREFACE

The books in this series offer introductions to major critical thinkers who have influenced literary studies and the humanities. The *Routledge Critical Thinkers* series provides the books you can turn to first when a new name or concept appears in your studies.

Each book will equip you to approach a key thinker's original texts by explaining her or his key ideas, putting them into context and, perhaps most importantly, showing you why this thinker is considered to be significant. The emphasis is on concise, clearly written guides which do not presuppose a specialist knowledge. Although the focus is on particular figures, the series stresses that no critical thinker ever existed in a vacuum but, instead, emerged from a broader intellectual, cultural and social history. Finally, these books will act as a bridge between you and the thinker's original texts: not replacing them but rather complementing what she or he wrote.

These books are necessary for a number of reasons. In his 1997 autobiography, *Not Entitled*, the literary critic Frank Kermode wrote of a time in the 1960s:

> On beautiful summer lawns, young people lay together all night, recovering from their daytime exertions and listening to a troupe of Balinese musicians. Under their blankets or their sleeping bags, they would chat drowsily about the gurus of the time ... What they repeated was largely hearsay; hence my

lunchtime suggestion, quite impromptu, for a series of short, very cheap books offering authoritative but intelligible introductions to such figures.

There is still a need for 'authoritative and intelligible introductions'. But this series reflects a different world from the 1960s. New thinkers have emerged and the reputations of others have risen and fallen, as new research has developed. New methodologies and challenging ideas have spread through arts and humanities. The study of literature is no longer – if it ever was – simply the study and evaluation of poems, novels and plays. It is also the study of ideas, issues, and difficulties which arise in any literary text and in its interpretation. Other arts and humanities subjects have changed in analogous ways.

With these changes, new problems have emerged. The ideas and issues behind these radical changes in the humanities are often presented without reference to wider contexts or as theories which you can simply 'add on' to the texts you read. Certainly, there's nothing wrong with picking out selected ideas or using what comes to hand – indeed, some thinkers have argued that this is, in fact, all we can do. However, it is sometimes forgotten that each new idea comes from the pattern and development of somebody's thought and it is important to study the range and context of their ideas. Against theories 'floating in space', the *Routledge Critical Thinkers* series places key thinkers and their ideas firmly back in their contexts.

More than this, these books reflect the need to go back to the thinker's own texts and ideas. Every interpretation of an idea, even the most seemingly innocent one, offers its own 'spin', implicitly or explicitly. To read only books on a thinker, rather than texts by that thinker, is to deny yourself a chance of making up your own mind. Sometimes what makes a significant figure's work hard to approach is not so much its style or content as the feeling of not knowing where to start. The purpose of these books is to give you a 'way in' by offering an accessible overview of these thinkers' ideas and works and by guiding your further reading, starting with each thinker's own texts. To use a metaphor from the philosopher Ludwig Wittgenstein (1889–1951), these books are ladders, to be thrown away after you have climbed to the next level. Not only, then, do they equip you to approach new ideas, but also they empower you, by leading you back to the theorist's own texts and encouraging you to develop your own informed opinions.

Finally, these books are necessary because, just as intellectual needs have changed, the education systems around the world – the contexts in which introductory books are usually read – have changed radically, too. What was suitable for the minority higher education system of the 1960s is not suitable for the larger, wider, more diverse, high technology education systems of the twenty-first century. These changes call not just for new, up-to-date, introductions but new methods of presentation. The presentational aspects of *Routledge Critical Thinkers* have been developed with today's students in mind.

Each book in the series has a similar structure. They begin with a section offering an overview of the life and ideas of each thinker and explain why she or he is important. The central section of each book discusses the thinker's key ideas, their context, evolution and reception. Each book concludes with a survey of the thinker's impact, outlining how their ideas have been taken up and developed by others. In addition, there is a detailed final section suggesting and describing books for further reading. This is not a 'tacked-on' section but an integral part of each volume. In the first part of this section you will find brief descriptions of the thinker's key works, then, following this, information on the most useful critical works and, in some cases, on relevant websites. This section will guide you in your reading, enabling you to follow your interests and develop your own projects. Throughout each book, references are given in what is known as the Harvard system (the author and the date of a work cited are given in the text and you can look up the full details in the bibliography at the back). This offers a lot of information in very little space. The books also explain technical terms and use boxes to describe events or ideas in more detail, away from the main emphasis of the discussion. Boxes are also used at times to highlight definitions of terms frequently used or coined by a thinker. In this way, the boxes serve as a kind of glossary, easily identified when flicking through the book.

The thinkers in the series are 'critical' for three reasons. First, they are examined in the light of subjects which involve criticism: principally literary studies or English and cultural studies, but also other disciplines which rely on the criticism of books, ideas, theories and unquestioned assumptions. Second, studying their work will provide you with a 'tool kit' for your own informed critical reading and thought, which will heighten your own criticism. Third, these thinkers are critical because they are crucially important: they deal with ideas and questions which can overturn conventional understandings of the world, of texts, of everything we take for granted, leaving us with a deeper understanding of what we already knew and with new ideas.

No introduction can tell you everything. However, by offering a way into critical thinking, this series hopes to begin to engage you in an activity which is productive, constructive and potentially life-changing.

ACKNOWLEDGEMENTS

My principal debt is to Claire Colebrook, who read successive drafts of the manuscript, and offered many valuable comments. When writing the book I was particularly grateful for the friendship and wit of Ali Lumsden, Tanja Rähneberg, Martin Reid, Steve Cramer, Penny Fielding and James Loxley. The book is dedicated to my parents, Paula and Keith.

Author and publishers wish to acknowledge Faber and Faber Ltd for permission to reproduce 'Sunday Morning' from Wallace Stevens' *Collected Poems*.

WHY NIETZSCHE?

Despite the fact that he was a late-nineteenth-century thinker, Friedrich Nietzsche (1844–1900) provided arguments that challenge and undermine many of the assumptions that we still hold dear today. It is difficult for us to imagine a world without common sense, the distinction between truth and falsehood, the belief in some form of morality or an agreement that we are all human. But Nietzsche did imagine such a world and he also argued that we should write and think in such a way that we would realise this world. Nietzsche was not just another philosopher or thinker: he challenged the very concepts of knowledge and thought. More importantly, he insisted that through transforming how we write and think we might transform who we are.

Nietzsche's philosophy insists that we ask questions about a range of issues that we assume to be matters of common sense. Whereas most philosophers are content to find a place for themselves within the received history of thought by analysing and refining the function of concepts, Nietzsche posed the radical questions: What is thought for? What does it mean to 'think' and how is thinking related to other forces within life? When we say that our culture and way of life reflect our 'values', how do we create values and how do they express the way we do or should live? We assume, he explained, that humanity is born with an innate moral sense and that truth is an objective and ideal standard by which we regulate our ideas and actions. But what if we discovered that 'morality' is the historical effect of regimes of cruelty, violence and force and that 'truth' is merely a particular perspective we impose upon life in order to render it explicable in moral terms? Could we possibly conceive of a way of living beyond the moral dichotomy of good and evil? And if we could do so, what might such a life look like?

BIOGRAPHICAL BACKGROUND

Nietzsche was born in Rocken, Saxony, in 1844, the son of a Lutheran pastor. His father died when he was a child, and Nietzsche, his mother, two maiden aunts and his younger sister Elizabeth (who was to assume considerable importance in her brother's life and the reception of his work) moved to Naumburg in 1850. Nietzsche left for boarding school in Pforza in 1858, where he established himself as a brilliant and precocious scholar, then studied classical philology at Bonn and Leipzig Universities, and in 1869 was appointed Extraordinary Professor of Classical Philology at Basel University, aged only 24. His first book, *The Birth of Tragedy from the Spirit of Music*, was published three years later. Already Nietzsche's idiosyncratic and combative style was evident: his book offers a visionary overview of the origins and decline of Greek tragic culture, and claims that this culture was destroyed by the subordination of the poetic imagination to a sterile rationalism that has come to dominate our own modern age. This provocative thesis was delivered in fewer than 120 pages devoid of footnotes or substantial scholarly references. Notwithstanding its brevity, *The Birth of Tragedy* expressed two of Nietzsche's most enduring themes, each of which was wholly at odds with the political disengagement and intellectual conservatism of the German university system. Nietzsche suggests first that 'philosophy' and 'culture' are *not* rarefied and elevated pursuits, but rather the expressions of a ceaseless competition between conflicting forces and drives. Secondly, he argues that we are mistaken in understanding philosophy to be a comprehensive and abstract account of dominant concepts and ideas; instead, the proper task of philosophy should be to identify and promote those historical forces that embody a 'strong' and creative movement of life and to recreate those forces in the present. Not surprisingly, *The Birth of Tragedy* was fiercely condemned by the academic community for its 'unphilosophical' approach, although the shock that Nietzsche's work produced in intellectual circles was represented in more neutral terms as distaste for his violation of scholarly etiquette, abrupt shifts of historical focus and needlessly polemical tone. The stage was set for a dispute between Nietzsche and German intellectual culture that was to last the rest of his life.

This initial bout of hostility was followed by a disrespectful silence on the part of his critics. Consequently, the dozen or so books Nietzsche completed in the next sixteen years made little or no impression upon the general reading public, despite their incendiary content. He continued to teach at Basel until 1879, when he was forced to retire because of ill health precipitated, it now appears, by his contraction of syphilis in the late 1860s. From this point, Nietzsche led the life of an independent thinker, devoting himself to a furious schedule of writing, earning little money, and moving constantly between hot and cooler climates as his health dictated. Although Nietzsche's peripatetic existence outside the academy is frequently interpreted as a typically individualist and nonconformist gesture, it may also be understood as part of a more general historical movement: the separation of radical thinkers from establishment intellectual communities. This schism was a consequence of the collapse of revolutionary hopes and the dream of a new society after the failed marzrevolution of March 1848, a year of revolutionary turmoil across Europe (Magnus and Higgins 1996: 74).

The failure of the marzrevolution was a turning point in nineteenth-century German history. The aims of the rebellion were political and economic reform, the unity of the various German states, free parliamentary elections, freedom of the press, a written constitution and the establishment of a Bill of Rights. The rebellion was precipitated by a number of factors: the example set by the revolutionary assaults on autocracy represented by the American Revolution of 1776, the French Revolution of 1789, and the subsequent French rebellions of July 1830 and February 1848; the emergence of a large and immiserated industrial working class; the domestic political repression exemplified by the military response to the 1844 rebellion of Silesian weavers in search of cheaper food and better wages; and the famine and starvation produced by the crop failures of 1847. It was initially successful, leading to major concessions by the Prussian King Friedrich Wilhelm IV, but lost momentum because of disputes between its liberal and radical factions and the counter-rebellion of the Prussian aristocracy (backed up by the military). In April 1849 the king was offered the crown of emperor under a new constitution. The new parliament inaugurated by the rebels gradually disintegrated and the old monarchical and feudal order was re-established. From this point radical thinkers and those critical of the existing order redirected their energies away from mainstream political culture and participation in the state's institutions, and began to develop alternative traditions of politics and philosophy.

As we will see, Nietzsche had little time for the democratic and egalitarian objectives of the radicals and reformers, but joined them in finding the conservatism of German culture and politics stultifying. He therefore embraced a nomadic existence for the last ten sane years of his life, wandering extensively through Germany, Switzerland, France and Italy, while he maintained his assault upon modern thinking and living. While in Turin in January 1889 he experienced a complete mental collapse, from which he never recovered. He was delivered over to the care of his sister and mother, with whom he lived for the next eleven years in a state of almost complete prostration until his death on 25 August 1900.

NIETZSCHE'S CHALLENGE

The challenge of Nietzsche's work consists in the questions he poses concerning the meaning and value of life. Nietzsche felt compelled to pose these questions because he believed that modern life was characterised by a fateful form of 'nihilism'. Nietzsche employed the term 'nihilism' to describe the sense of emptiness or 'nothingness' befalling a people that had no faith in the standards and values that regulated its daily life, but who could find no way to bring new values into being. The problem for humanity today, he argued, is that it no longer believes in the moral ideals that shaped the Christian view of the world, but lacks the power to create values capable of underpinning a new vision of life. All around him Nietzsche saw men and women who could no longer believe in the transcendent value of Christian divinity, but felt unable to dispense with the rules and prohibitions of Christian morality. As he wrote in *Twilight of the Idols*, first published in German in 1889, 'They have got rid of the Christian God, and now feel obliged to cling all the more to Christian morality' (1990b: 80).

Nietzsche's famous declaration in *The Gay Science*, first published in German in 1882, of the 'death of God' was intended to alert humanity to this 'twilight of the Idols' and to underline the necessity of producing an interpretation of life unconstrained by the Christian inheritance.

What distinguishes Nietzsche from other nineteenth-century critics of religion, morality and nineteenth-century life is that he does not search for a more effective moral life; he attempts to save life *from* morality itself. He argues that nineteenth-century culture experiences life as a form of nihilism because it has invented a series of moral concepts such as 'truth', 'selflessness' and 'equality' that have been raised above life in order to regulate and judge life. Not only do these moral values repress what Nietzsche took to be the most profound instinctual forces of life; they also encourage us to live *reactively* according to an inflexible and timeless moral law instead of creating our values *actively* for ourselves. For Nietzsche, the moral circumscription of life evacuated thought of positive content. 'Morality is merely sign-language, merely symptomatology,' he complained; 'one must already know *what* it is about to derive profit from it' (1990b: 66). He worked tirelessly against what we might call the 'transcendence' of thought: the subjection of life to concepts that determine the form and content of life. Instead, he sought to develop a principle of life that was *interior* to life and which might enable him to forge a connection between the most powerful forces of existence and the creation of new values.

Nietzsche discovered this new principle of life in his theory of the will to power. He claimed that life is driven forward by an inhuman principle of creation that is *immanent* or interior to life: we should not *judge* life from the point of view of an external morality, but *live* life to its maximum potential. Will to power is an inhuman principle because it envisages *all* life, not just human life, as united by a common striving for power. The entirety of existence is perceived as a ceaseless process of becoming and transformation within which each form of life seeks to expand and increase its power. The aim of life from this perspective is not enlightenment, moral improvement or even self-preservation; it inheres in the acquisition of power. A particular form of life becomes powerful insofar as it appropriates other forces to its domain. Every movement of life bears within it a configuration of forces. The struggle between powers produces a hierarchy of stronger and weaker forces, which then leads to the creation of concepts. Indeed, what we rather euphemistically call 'values' describe the domination of a particular perspective upon or interpretation of life – such as the 'ascetic ideal' of Christian moralism or the interests of the ruling class – at a determinate historical conjuncture. There is, Nietzsche asserts, no 'world' or 'essence' that we can know *behind* this competition of forces; every concept and value we possess represents the triumph of a powerful interpretation of life. The moral image of humanity only appeared because we invented a language to project our values on to the world and create it in our own image and then promptly forgot that we had invented this image for ourselves. In contrast, Nietzsche presents a challenge to the moral interpretation of existence by marking its historical emergence and limits and developing an 'immoral' or non-moral image of thought to replace it.

Nietzsche's challenge to the moral image of 'man' led him to develop a genealogical critique of the history of our moral values. He rejected both the idea of morality as an innate or natural human capacity and the identification of the origin and purpose of moral practices proposed by traditional historians. Instead, he focused upon the material forces that produce moral concepts in the first place. For Nietzsche, moral concepts such as 'conscience', 'guilt' and 'humility' are produced by successive reinterpretations of life created by dominant historical forces and interests. Every reinterpretation expresses a specific quantity of will to power. Some of Nietzsche's most striking passages detail the secret desire for mastery inscribed within the sacrificial rhetoric of Christian asceticism (the purging and denial of the self opposed to the accumulation of worldly possessions). Because every historical interpretation of life is produced by the victory of strong over weaker forces, Nietzsche argued that we should abandon our idealistic notion of history as an objective account or a narrative of moral development. The point of historical inquiry from what he referred to as a *genealogical* perspective is rather to separate ascending from descending modes of life and to create a version of the past that enables us to develop the most vital and powerful forces of the present.

NIETZSCHE'S POLITICS

Nietzsche's 'revaluation of all values', which relies upon a division between 'stronger' and 'weaker' forms of life, introduces the notorious issue of his politics. Nietzsche has long been caricatured as a fascistic thinker whose ideas found their eventual expression in the genocidal racial politics of Nazi Germany. In fact, Nietzsche despised nationalism and anti-Semitism and railed against the backwardness of the German Reich from the 1870s onwards. A good deal of the damage done to his reputation was inflicted by his sister Elizabeth Nietzsche (1846–1935), who assumed editorship of Nietzsche's corpus of work after his collapse into insanity in 1889. Elizabeth's political sympathies may be gauged by her marriage to the anti-Semitic political leader Bernhard Förster (1843–89). Her editorship of Nietzsche's work corrupted its content, removed many of the philosophical contexts that gave it its meaning, and prepared it for its appropriation by Nazi ideologues after Nietzsche's death in 1900.

However, Nietzsche's politics remain highly controversial even when Elizabeth Förster-Nietzsche's intervention is taken into account. This is true, in part, because he resolutely opposes our commonplace assumption of a moral context for political thought, whether that context takes the form of the Judaeo-Christian tradition or the egalitarian impulse of socialism and modern liberal democracy. Nietzsche opposed these movements because he believed that by positing the ideal of a general human nature or the appeal to equal rights, Christian morality, socialism and liberalism represented a triumph of base and slavish nature over the strong and independent spirit. In contrast, Nietzsche's 'aristocratic' or 'great politics' argued that the aim of culture and politics was to produce the 'Overman', a superior mode of being that knows only affirmation and creates its own values from the superabundance of its power:

> The problem I raise here is not what ought to succeed mankind in the sequence of species (– the human being is a *conclusion* –): but what type of human being one ought to *breed*, ought to *will*, as more valuable, more worthy of life, more certain of the future. This more valuable type has existed often enough already: but as a lucky accident, as an exception, never as *willed*.
>
> (1990b: 128)

Nietzsche's intemperate remarks about slavish natures, the 'weak' and women undoubtedly disclose a violent and troubling aspect of his imagination, and have contributed considerably to the misreading and avoidance of his work. So have his remarks about 'breeding' a higher type of being, although Nietzsche consistently employs the term in the context of an ethical and political, rather than biological, progression beyond the moral image of humanity. It is indisputable that Nietzsche's work can be appropriated for violent political ends, although this is also true of Christianity, egalitarian politics and the cultural humanism that underpinned the 'civilising mission' of colonial imperialism. The *risk* of Nietzsche's antifoundationalist mode of thought – a style of thinking that takes us beyond foundational concepts like 'morality', 'good', 'evil' and 'justice' – is that it opens up new ways of thinking about being, responsibility, ethics and what it means to be human. To say that such thought may present a grave risk to what is glibly known as the 'human condition' is not, of course, to say that this risk is *necessarily* one of violence or that Nietzsche's provocative diagnosis of modern culture should be ignored. One of the greatest challenges to contemporary thought may well be to develop Nietzsche's insights upon value, morality, politics and ethics outside some of the more reductive contexts that inform his work.

ART

Another important and recurrent Nietzschean theme concerns the power of art. Throughout his writings, he challenges the subordination of our perceptions and intuitions to a pre-established and normative idea of truth. He discerns this reactive gesture in various guises. The creative and life-embracing aristocratic spirit that is capable of forming concepts is domesticated and weakened by being submitted to the criteria of truth: accuracy, consistency and reasonableness. The repression of intuition and perception for the sake of truth then forms the basis for the linguistic division of the endless becoming of life into a 'subject' (the consciousness of 'man') and an 'object' (the external world). Nietzsche claims that it is by judging the flux of life according to human concepts that we create the idea of a universal human nature. In contrast, he insists that the fixed concepts we employ to establish the universal truth of human nature and its relation to the world originate in poetic metaphors, the origin of which we have forgotten. The force of art for Nietzsche is that it attends to the *singularity* of our perception of the world before it is assimilated into fixed concepts and values. In so doing, art reminds us of the *metaphorical* origins of our conceptual systems and suggests other ways in which the relationship between subjects and objects may be understood. Because the concepts that we inherit determine our idea of the 'human', the radical promise of art is that it might create a future for life beyond the exhausted and moralised image of modern humanity. The promise of an aesthetic transformation of life beyond any moral determination lies at the heart of Nietzsche's work, and defines his image as the first 'post-human' thinker in an age in which the concept of the 'human' was in profound and protracted crisis.

THIS BOOK

The 'Key Ideas' section of this book examines Nietzsche's critique of the decadence and nihilism of modern 'man' and his attempt to develop a new style of thinking and living. It begins with Nietzsche's examination of the rise and decline of Greek tragedy and aristocratic values, and the beginning of his quest for a non-moral style of thought. The next three chapters consider Nietzsche's analysis of the origin and constitution of truth and his genealogical reading of the development of our moral values. Chapter 5 explores Nietzsche's ethical and political theory in more detail, and introduces crucial terms such as *ressentiment*, nihilism and slave morality. Chapter 6 examines his conception of the 'Overman' as a representative of a new ethics of affirmation beyond good and evil. The final chapter provides an introduction to Nietzsche's theory of will to power in the context of his inhuman philosophy of force, interpretation and perspective.

KEY IDEAS

KEY IDEAS

1

TRAGEDY

Nietzsche's first book, *The Birth of Tragedy out of the Spirit of Music*, first published in German in 1872, occupies a curious position in the development of his thought. It is here that he introduces a series of concepts and distinctions that have become definitive of a 'Nietzschean' style of thinking. In fewer than 120 pages, Nietzsche redefines the relation between art, science and philosophy, and marks a distinction between the proper and improper use of history for the production of 'strong' values. *The Birth of Tragedy* also introduces a creative antagonism between the forces of Apollo (God of sunlight, order and harmony) and Dionysius (God of wine, revel and disorder) that became central to his work. He then goes on to deliver a number of remarks about democracy, modernity and the modern 'rabble' that have defined his image in the popular imagination. Fourteen years later, however, in his 'Attempt at a Self-Criticism', Nietzsche condemns *The Birth of Tragedy* as an 'impossible' and 'fanatical' book and retracts two of its most celebrated claims, namely that tragedy offers us a 'new art of metaphysical consolation' for the terrors of existence, and that the modern German spirit, personified by the composer Richard Wagner (1813–88), represents the culmination and realisation of the Greek genius.

The compositional history of *The Birth of Tragedy* makes clear an important aspect of Nietzsche's intellectual style. His philosophy is not 'systematic' in the sense that its earliest insights and ideas are gradually developed into a completely coherent vision of the world. Instead, Nietzsche's writing expresses a form of passionate argument that continually examines and revises its main propositions according to their power to extend the creative capacity of a particular form of life. To make sense of Nietzsche's work, then, we need to replace traditional concerns about the *consistency* of a philosophical corpus with a series of questions about what makes a text or position *possible and necessary* at this particular stage in his development. For example, why would a philosopher with such a polemical attitude to modernity choose to address this issue by means of a discussion of Greek tragedy, and what statements about history and cultural value did it enable him to make? And what did Nietzsche find significant in classical Greek culture to make this discussion valuable in the first place?

To begin with the first question, Nietzsche is interested in tragedy because it offers the supreme example of an art form that provides insight into the *strength* and *weakness* of a culture. The experience of tragedy, he argues, forces a culture to reconsider or revalue its values; and Nietzsche notes later that *'Birth of Tragedy* was my first revaluation of all values' (1990b: 121). Tragic art compels such a revaluation because it yields a profound insight into the depth and terror of human experience. It does so by teaching us that humanity's potential to develop a vital and expansive existence is fundamentally linked to its capacity to endure suffering and terror. The Greeks, Nietzsche argues, developed a tragic art because they had the strength to envisage life as a continuous cycle of creation and destruction. This vision required strength because it affirmed the *whole* of life – including violence, struggle and conquest – instead of celebrating merely its most elevated and 'civilised' manifestations. The importance of tragic art for Nietzsche is that it enabled the Greeks to experience the chaos and force of a thoroughly pre-cultural and inhuman form of life. Tragedy expressed some of the most profound and vital aspects of what to means to be human – the lust for power and dominion, the primal force of sexuality, the desire to smash outmoded structures and create a new vision of the world – that we have subsequently repressed in order to become civilised beings. Indeed, the later experience of Greek tragedy puts into question what we think of as 'moral' and 'civilised' values and forces us to consider the types of value we must *create* in order to develop a powerful, dynamic and expansive way of life.

TRAGEDY, ART AND CULTURE

The philosophical question of which values a culture should strive to develop had important historical and political dimensions for Nietzsche. *The Birth of Tragedy* was composed during the Franco-German war of 1870–1. For Nietzsche, this conflict of nation-states, combined with the simultaneous rise of both socialism and political nationalism, represented a crisis of European cultural confidence. His response to this crisis, as we will see in Chapter 5, was to call for an aristocratic or 'great' politics that rejected the idea of equal rights and the claims of national identity in order to privilege only the most vital and powerful forces within a culture. This aristocratic politics, he claimed, was the driving force behind ancient Greek society, art and culture. Nietzsche also saw in Greek life a potential solution to the question posed by the malaise of modern culture and politics: what is the value of existence? Why was it, he asks, that the most beautiful and accomplished race of mankind was the one to develop a specifically *tragic* art? Nietzsche saw no contradiction in this state of affairs. He suggests, instead, that the ability to embrace the extreme pessimism of tragedy was the quality that enabled the genius of Greek culture to emerge:

> Is there a pessimism of strength? An intellectual predilection for what is hard, terrible, evil, problematic in existence, arising from well-being, overflowing health, the abundance of existence? Is it perhaps possible to suffer from over-abundance? A tempting and challenging, sharp-eyed courage that craves the terrible as one can crave the enemy, the worthy enemy, against whom it can test its strength?

> (1993: 3–4)

Nietzsche's radical redefinition of Greek cultural history makes a distinction between art and tragedy on the one hand and philosophy and science on the other. It is an intellectual commonplace, he contends, that the main burden of our inheritance from the Greeks is the glory of their achievements in philosophy and science. To conceive of Greek thought is to call to mind the moral philosophy of Socrates (470–399 BC), the new cosmology of Plato's (427–347 BC) *Timaeus*, Aristotle's (384–322 BC) reformulation of scientific method in his *Posterior Analytics* and Pythagoras' (*c.* 560–480 BC) revolutionary innovations in mathematics. Intellectual events like these created a fundamental rupture in the history of western thought, and placed new ideas of reason, morality and logic at the heart of intellectual endeavour. Yet it was precisely these accomplishments, Nietzsche argues, that represent the *eclipse*, rather than the apotheosis, of classical Greek culture. For what is the purpose of establishing the supremacy of abstract and ideal conceptions of morality, reason and logic except to 'ward off the image of every-thing terrible, evil, cryptic, destructive and deadly underlying exist-ence' (1993: 6)? This sequestration of 'reason' and 'morality' from an experience of inhuman and destructive forces cut Hellenic thought off from the total economy of life. Moreover, it is this weakened and restricted notion of life – a notion of life defined by rational and moral norms – that we have inherited from the Greeks and that forms the basis for our modern ideas of moral and cultural value. Now we have ideas *about* life (such as democracy, egalitarianism or moral virtue) rather than experiencing the radical force of life that was kept alive by the Greek tragic spirit. Humanity has never been so 'moral' and so 'healthy', Nietzsche laments, and yet it has never been so neurotic either. Might we not then conclude, in the face of all 'modern ideas' and the preju-dice of democratic taste, that 'the victory of *optimism*, the now predominant *reason*, practical and theoretical *utilitarianism*, like democ-racy itself, with which it is coeval, is a symptom of waning power, of approaching senescence, of physiological fatigue'? (p. 7).

Nietzsche's response to this melancholy history is fundamentally to transform our perception of the relationship between *being* and *value*. One of the principal problems of modern culture, he argues, is that a form of life is judged according to is capacity to conform to certain moral norms. These normative moral standards may be embodied in religious appeals to charity and forbearance, or political calls for equal rights and social democracy; what all such norms share is the percep-tion of a common and universal set of values that gives human life its meaning and justification. But instead of judging life from the point of view of morality, Nietzsche declares, we need to determine the value of morality from the perspective of *life* (1993: 7). This insistence explains his life-long fascination with Greek tragic art. The genius of Greek tragedy, Nietzsche claims, lay in its capacity to open itself to the myriad force of life without adopting a moral perspective. Tragedy, in Nietzschean terms, forms the basis for a *non-moral* vision of life. Conversely, the demise of Greek tragedy occurred when life was sub-jected to an explicitly moral evaluation. 'Morality' in *The Birth of Tragedy* is the product of a decadent *interpretation* of life that accompanies the destruction of Greek tragic culture. This tragic culture was destroyed when the Greeks no longer had the strength to affirm the inhuman and destructive power of life. Instead, they raised a number of abstract concepts above life in order to regulate its chaotic force. The most pernicious of these concepts, Nietzsche argues, was morality. The destruction of Greek tragedy arrives, then, with the production of an idea of life (the 'moral life') that is turned against life. In contrast, Nietzsche joins with the ancient Greeks in asserting that 'the existence of the world is justified only as an aesthetic phenomenon' (p. 8). The power of tragic art – indeed, all art – for Nietzsche lies in its expression of a profound 'counter-moral tendency' that refuses to subordinate life to conceptual fictions like 'morality' and 'truth', or endorse a division between reason and truth on one hand, and art and falsehood on the other. Instead, Nietzsche's Greek tragic art challenges all values hostile to life by affirming a vision of existence 'based on appearance, art, deception, point of view, the necessity of perspective and error' (p. 8). The noblest mode of life is not submission to universal moral norms; it is rather, as Nietzsche wrote in *The Gay Science*, to give aesthetic shape to our character by surveying all that our nature presents of strength and weakness and then moulding it into 'an artistic plan' until each of our aspects is integrated into a powerful expression of personality (1974: 232). Art is thereby transformed into the highest principle of existence by revealing the multiple ways that life comes into being. Art gives a purposive shape to experience in the active creation of values.

The 'revaluation' of life implicit in Nietzsche's particular view of tragedy may be illustrated by reference to one of the most famous Greek tragedies: Sophocles' (496–*c*.413 BC) *Oedipus Rex*. The play tells of the tragic fall of Oedipus, King of Thebes. When the play begins, Thebes is in turmoil: the harvests have failed, and the gods have abandoned the city. In desperation, Oedipus asks Creon, his wife's brother, to consult Apollo and attempt to discover the reason for their calamitous state. Creon returns with the news that Thebes has been stricken because the murderers of its former ruler, Laius – whose wife, Jocasta, Oedipus has subsequently married – have never been brought to account. Oedipus immediately proclaims that he will dispel the plague upon Thebes by finding and banishing the miscreant. Indeed, Oedipus declares, were the murderer to be discovered hiding in his own palace, he would be prepared to share this awful punishment. From this point Oedipus' fate unravels with terrifying rapidity. First, he is informed by the blind seer Tiresias that the man he seeks is not just Laius' murderer: he is also Laius' son, who will go on to marry his own mother. Then he is told the worst news of all: the man he seeks is no other than himself! Oedipus' furious insistence that the facts of this matter do not match his own case – he was born the son of Polybus, King of Corinth, and his father has recently died of natural causes – is insufficient to avert his tragic destiny. For it gradually emerges that Oedipus was in fact fathered by Laius, only to be abandoned on a hillside in fear of a prophecy that he would live to kill his own father. Spared by a gentle shepherd, he was taken to Corinth, where he was raised within the royal household. The rest is too awfully predictable: dealt with discourteously by Laius at an isolated crossroads, Oedipus strikes and kills his own father. He compounds this horror by marrying Jocasta, his own mother, in fulfilment of the prophecy. The appalling revelation of Oedipus' true identity leads Jocasta to hang herself and Oedipus to put out his own eyes. The play ends in this mood of unremitting bleakness by depicting the fragility of human existence and the pitilessness of fate.

The traditional response to Oedipus' fall is that it offers us a terrifying moral lesson in the consequences of overstepping the boundaries to human ambition set by the gods. The tragedy presents the dark knowledge that the pattern of our life is determined by a divinely ordained destiny or 'fate', which we are powerless to alter. The most famous expression of this view is Aristotle's interpretation of tragedy as a form that generates pity and fear in order to purge mankind of its attraction to the destructive power of life by 'the sacrifice of the hero in the interest of a moral view of the world' (1993: 107). In modern times, following the pyschoanalytic theories of Sigmund Freud (1856–1939), Oedipus' tragedy has been transformed into an individual 'complex' and rewritten as a bourgeois family drama. Thus Freud argued that every boy imagines himself to be his mother's lover and consequently wishes to kill his paternal rival. However, the father's presence looms large as a pervasive threat of violence and castration. Accordingly, the boy learns to repress his Oedipal desire for his mother, identify with his father's role, and accept his future responsibilities as a worker and head of the family. In both of these readings, 'fate' has a moral meaning: fate is an order to be obeyed or a structure to which we ought to reconcile ourselves. For Nietzsche, however, fate is ruthless, meaningless, inhuman and excessively forceful. The inhuman ferocity of fate dominates the tragedy of Oedipus, where destiny is utterly destructive of the moral and familial order.

Nietzsche's reading of Greek art works explicitly against a moral reading of tragedy that would merely describe tragedy as an interplay of personalities. He insists, instead, that tragedy stages a violent confrontation between our most powerful drives and passions that takes us far beyond the fictions of the 'moral individual'. Tragedy is best understood neither as a hero's conflict with social forces nor as a personal Oedipal complex. For Nietzsche, the tragedy of Oedipus awakens us to inhuman natural forces that shatter our preconceived ideas about the value of 'knowledge' and 'morality'. He argues that Oedipus' experiences provide him with a fateful insight into the most sacred mysteries of nature. By solving the riddle posed by the Sphinx and thereby saving Thebes from destruction, Oedipus has 'clairvoyant' and 'magical' powers conferred upon him that allow him to overcome mankind's separation from nature and the inhuman realm of the gods (1993: 47). However, the wisdom that Oedipus acquires also represents an 'abominable crime against nature' because he triumphed over the Sphinx by breaking the 'spell of the past and the future' that fate casts over mankind. To break this spell is to destroy the 'rigid law of individuation' that enables every human being to detach itself from the chaotic flux of nature and constitute itself as an autonomous and moral form of life. By overcoming the Sphinx, Oedipus refuses to see life as something that happens to 'us' according to the iron law of fate; rather, he becomes one with the force of life by affirming his sovereign will over every external law and prohibition. Oedipus therefore becomes more than human by defying the moral law. This, for Nietzsche, is the tragic paradox of Oedipus' story: he can only experience the supreme force of life at the moment that his moral individuality is rendered meaningless. The tragic dissolution of Oedipus' moral being manifests itself to us in his two terrible crimes against nature – incest and parricide – that destroy his moral universe and leave him an outcast and exile.

Oedipus the King, then, discloses a vision of the inhuman power of life that exceeds and threatens the moral evaluation of 'man'. Its mythic reconciliation of humanity with the subjugated and repressed force of nature is described by Nietzsche as the *Dionysiac* function of tragedy. However, this vision of the power of amoral and inhuman natural being has the potential to overwhelm humanity and render its existence petty and futile. The genius of Greek tragedy, for Nietzsche, was to preserve the memory of our primal and pre-moral bond with nature within an aesthetic form – the narratives, characters and images of tragic drama – that represented these primal energies in *human* terms. This is what Nietzsche called the 'magical' and *Apollonian* function of tragic art: the aesthetic structuring and reproduction of amoral natural forces in order that we might transcend the moral interpretation of existence:

> Sophocles saw the most suffering character on the Greek stage, the unhappy Oedipus, as the noble man who is predestined for error and misery despite his wisdom, but who finally, through his terrible suffering, exerts a magical and beneficial power that continues to prevail after his death. The noble man does not sin, the profound poet wishes to tell us: through his actions every law, every natural order, the whole moral world can be destroyed, and through the actions a higher magic circle of effects is drawn, founding a new world on the ruin of the old, now destroyed.

(1993: 46)

APOLLO AND DIONYSIUS

The two major concepts introduced in *The Birth of Tragedy* are the Apollonian and the Dionysiac. Nietzsche begins by arguing that 'art derives its continuous development from the duality of the Apolline and the Dionysiac' (1993: 14). Apollo represents the capacity for order, clarity, proportion and formal harmony within the Greek spirit. This power reaches its apotheosis in Greek sculpture and visual art; but it also manifests itself in the classical desire to treat the self as a work of art and develop a strong well-shaped character. Apollo therefore represents a divine image of the *principium individuationis*: the well-fashioned character who stands apart from the multitude (p. 16). In contrast, Dionysius represents a state of chaotic and ecstatic energy which threatens the integrity of every formal structure. The cult of Dionysius celebrates sexuality, unconscious desire and the amorality of natural forces; it seeks to destroy the cultivated 'individuation' of the autonomous individual and reunite us with the 'innermost core' of nature (p. 76). The Dionysiac finds aesthetic expression in the primal force and narcotic rhythms of music, which intoxicate the listener into a 'complete forgetting of the self' (p. 17).

Apollonian art has, for Nietzsche, both a formal and an ethical character. The formal features of order and clarity possess an ethical dimension because they enable us to structure undifferentiated reality into coherent narratives and to reflect upon the nature of our experience. The ethical aspect of Apollonian art becomes clear if we follow Nietzsche in returning the form to its origins in the physiological state of dream. The Apollonian begins in the 'beautiful illusion' of dream, Nietzsche argues, because dreams teach us the pleasure of the 'immediate apprehension of form' (1993: 15). This experience of aesthetic harmony is the pre-condition of all visual art. Apollonian art, like dream, is an 'illusion' because it provides a narrative form with which we can organise an undifferentiated series of drives into distinct images and statements. Nietzsche later describes dream as 'the illusion of illusion' (p. 25). He does so because, following the German philosopher Arthur Schopenhauer (1788–1860), he views the habitual concepts by which we structure our daily lives (such as time, space, causality and identity) as illusions or narrative fictions we impose upon the chaotic nature of experience. Because what we know as 'real' life is produced by this type of narrative illusion, it follows that dreams and visual art which offer a powerful second-order version of the real present the 'illusion of illusion'. Nietzsche consistently exalts the capacity of Apollonian art to concentrate formless nature into distinct images because it is by representing our experience to ourselves that we learn to question and transform our values. Apollonian art reveals to us the 'higher truth' of life as the active creation of new values and modes of existence; indeed, it is through this art that 'life is made possible and worth living' (p. 16).

However, despite the ethical privilege conferred upon the Apollonian in *The Birth of Tragedy*, Nietzsche insists that it must be complemented by Dionysiac energy. Nietzsche never wavers from his belief that by revealing the amorality of nature's character as a creative and destructive force – that nature is a powerful agent of change because it also delights in destruction – the Dionysiac presents the most profound insight possible into humanity's character as a natural being. Unless it incorporates the transfiguring power of Dionysiac energy, the Apollonian threatens to petrify life within dead forms. Consequently, the Apollonian and Dionysiac must exist in a mutually defining relationship with each other. Yet Nietzsche is also aware that the Dionysiac 'paroxysms of intoxication' ultimately destroy every cultural form that mankind develops to reflect upon its own values (1993: 18). The ecstatic state of Dionysiac music and ritual 'even seeks to destroy individuality and redeem it with a mystical sense of unity'. Therefore Apollonian aesthetic forms are required to structure Dionysiac energies. For this reason Nietzsche represents Apollonian art as a formal limit: it offers a 'restraining boundary' that prevents man's 'wilder impulses' from 'becoming pathological' (p. 16). The formal limit provided by Apollonian art enables man to separate himself from nature and constitute himself as an autonomous individual; it is this *principium individuationis* that permits him to develop social and cultural structures to regulate his existence (p. 17).

Nietzsche's elevation of the Apollonian over the Dionysiac in *The Birth of Tragedy* is apt to confuse readers familiar with his later celebration of Dionysius in books including *Thus Spoke Zarathustra*, first published in German in 1885 and *Ecce Homo*, written in 1888 and published posthumously in German in 1908. However, Nietzsche is not being inconsistent or self-contradictory in his use of these terms; instead, 'Apollonian' and 'Dionysiac' assume new and different meanings. The later Dionysius incorporates the Apollonian principle: to be 'Dionysiac' in Nietzsche's last books is to integrate all of one's drives and passions into a spontaneous and powerful self conceived as a well-fashioned aesthetic totality. The Dionysiac individual represents a harmonious and controlled expression of the superabundant force of life which needs no recourse to transcendent ideas raised above life in order to judge life. For this reason the primary antagonism of Nietzsche's mature work is not between Apollo and Dionysius, but between Dionysius and Christ, who interprets life in terms of absolute and timeless moral laws.

Western art and culture from the Greeks onward, Nietzsche argues, are produced by the 'struggle' and 'violent opposition' between the Apollonian and Dionysiac (1993: 14). The violent struggle between these two counter-balanced forces threatened at one point to tear the Greek world apart until they were compelled by a 'metaphysical miracle of the Hellenic will' to combine themselves within a single aesthetic form that could concentrate and develop their powers (p. 14). This aesthetic form was Greek tragedy. Before considering the origins of tragedy in more detail, we should note that the dynamic tension between the Apollonian and Dionysiac offers Nietzsche an explanatory model for the development and decline of Greek culture. This model enables

Nietzsche directly to confront the assumption implicit in the eighteenth-century German celebration of Greek culture of a connection between aesthetic form and national character. 'Given the incredible accuracy of their eyes, with their brilliant and frank delight in colour, we can hardly refrain', Nietzsche suggests, 'from assuming a logical causality of lines and contours, colours and groups, that puts later generations to shame, a sequence of scenes like those in their best reliefs' (p. 19). It is, however, a mistake, he continues, to understand this apotheosis of the Apollonian tendency in art as the 'natural' expression of the Greek character. Instead, the individuated form of Greek art was specifically developed to protect Greece from the 'dangerous force' of Dionysiac ritual sweeping the ancient world. 'It was in Doric art', Nietzsche contends, 'that Apollo's majestically repudiating stance was immortalized' (1993: 19). Apollonian art therefore establishes cultural order at the same time as it enables the expression of cultural values. Twentieth-century historians of ideas such as A. W. H. Adkins and Kimon Lycos have shown how Greek culture required forms of moral order as it moved from local, almost tribal, communities to city states. Nietzsche, however, sees this political and historical development as having a general relevance. The Greek example demonstrates that it is possible to live without an established, unquestioned and stable morality. The Greeks are exemplary in their ability to *create* values.

Nietzsche's dynamic reading of cultural development suggests that different epochs do not simply follow one another in a smooth natural progression. Instead, there are forces and conflicts within life which necessarily bring about destruction and reinvention. On this view, the aesthetic modulation between Apollo and Dionysius will be a continual process because Dionysiac energy possesses a force sufficient to bring any culture into crisis. Nietzsche identifies two specific consequences of this struggle between order and disorder: the development of Greek religion and the invention of the Greek gods. When the subversive power of Dionysiac ritual eventually entered the city, presenting a cultic and religious challenge to Greek civic order, the Greeks responded by developing a new aesthetic form capable of accommodating and structuring Dionysiac forces. This new form was a modified version of Greek religion. From this point, Greek religion organised itself around a ritualistic practice that ordered Dionysiac energies and offered a redemptive reading of its amoral combination of joy and suffering while systematically excluding the one element – music – that threatened to subvert social order. The particular danger posed by music is that 'the overwhelming power of sound, the unified flow of melody and the utterly incomparable power of harmony' produces a total liberation of all the forces of the body (the eyes, the limbs, the mouth and so on), and this dissolution of the body into specific sites of pleasure and pain destroys our sense of ourselves as autonomous and individuated social beings (1993: 20–1). The threatened dissolution of the autonomous self into a range of sensual forces and appetites was averted, Nietzsche argues, by the invention of the Olympian gods. The creation of these new deities was one of the great triumphs of Apollonian Greek art because it completed the reconfiguration of unruly Dionysian forces into an assertion of a coherent cultural identity begun by Greek religion. The gods are necessary for the Greeks because they represent an 'artistic *middle* world' where ecstatic and amoral Dionysiac life is embodied and contained within individuated images. They reveal a mode of existence in which 'everything is deified whether it be good or evil' (pp. 22, 23). The Greeks had an acute insight into the fear and horror of existence; they could only live with this knowledge by following the example of the gods they had themselves created, who turned the deepest suffering into joy and an affirmation of the creative possibilities of life. 'In order to live', Nietzsche concludes, 'the Greeks were powerfully compelled to create those gods' (p. 23).

TRAGIC ORIGINS

It is a fundamental premise of Nietzsche's dynamic conception of cultural history that the Greeks had constantly to recall the Dionysiac experience of self-annihilation in order that the redeeming vision of Apollonian art and autonomous selfhood could be born. The paradoxical pleasure we derive from tragic art does not originate in a moral decision to renounce overarching ambition (such as the hubris that leads individuals to challenge the gods or seek to usurp the king) and observe proper social limits; it is born, instead, from our *memory* of the Dionysiac force of life preserved for us in the perfection of Apollonian form. The story of the flourishing of Greek culture tells how 'the Dionysiac and the Apolline, in a sequence of mutually renewed births, mutually intensifying one another, dominated the nature of Greece' (1993: 27). The development of tragic art was crucial to this narrative because it provided a bridge between two worlds. Nietzsche detects the origins of tragic art in the Dionysian force of *music* and *lyric*. Lyric, he argues, was a musical force that existed before and beyond any modern idea of individualism. The lyric musician is at one with the primal contradiction and suffering of the world: he is himself 'nothing but primal suffering and its primal resonance' (p. 30). His identity emerged from the 'very depths' of being, and his lyrical images were merely an expression of the world that spoke through him. Nietzsche insists that the artist is not the ground or origin of aesthetic creation but the medium through which the primal force of life finds its most powerful and coherent expression. 'But in so far as the subject is an artist', he explains, 'he is already liberated from his individual will and has become a medium through which the only truly existent subject celebrates his redemption through illusion' (p. 32). Because art is a mediation of the primal force of Dionysius, and therefore does not originate in the self-reflection of the individual artist, we cannot claim that it has a moral or humanitarian function. The value of art is that it enables us to experience a creative force in life that exists *prior* to any moral or ideological interpretation we might impose upon it. Art is a force that exists beyond good and evil, which teaches us that our 'justification' lies in the discovery of new visions of what life might become.

MUSIC AND ILLUSION

Nietzsche's portrait of the artist as the privileged medium through whom 'life' speaks explains why music occupies a central role in his early philosophy. For music is not merely an expression of the 'primal oneness' of being: it is both being and the symbolisation of being in aesthetic form. Music, that is, expresses Dionysiac vitality, and yet the fact that it *represents* a type of being demonstrates its potential to discharge itself into an Apollonian symbolic form. Thus while what Nietzsche calls the 'world-symbolisation' of music exists 'beyond and prior to all phenomena' and can never be fully expressed by language, it also presents a type of symbolic narrative through which forms come into being (1993: 35). It is this *double* function of music as a Dionysiac force continually discharging itself into Apollonian images that makes it crucial to Nietzsche's theory of tragedy and which lies behind his celebrated claim that 'tragedy arose from the tragic chorus, and was originally only chorus and nothing else' (p. 36).

The tragic 'chorus' denotes the choral song from which tragic drama developed. It was originally a hymn sung by about fifty men, but by the time of the great tragic dramas of the fifth century BC it had dwindled to around fifteen actors. Its dramatic role varied historically: sometimes its vocal movement indicated a passage of time; at other times it explored the relation of man to the gods. Frequently the chorus offered a rhythmic counterpoint to the dramatic action, sometimes endorsing and sometimes challenging the sentiments of the tragic protagonists. Nietzsche's reading of the chorus dissents from those scholarly accounts that identify it as a representation of the views of the 'populace', the 'ideal viewer' or – worst of all – the 'moral law of the democratic Athenians' (1993: 36). Instead, the chorus represents in microcosm the entire tragic dynamic by which the overwhelming force of Dionysiac life is translated into a form that enables us to survive it with our sense of individuation intact. It does this by presenting a symbolic vision of the inexhaustible power of Dionysius and his unification with primal being by means of the 'middle world' of a narrative form. The choric production of a dramatic narrative performs a crucial function for the audience. The Dionysiac state affords humanity a terrifying glimpse into the chaos and meaningless of existence; by transforming this inhuman vision into images and ideas 'compatible with life', the chorus enables us to draw upon Dionysiac emergies while making the thought of life possible once again (p. 40). The simultaneous representation and dissipation of Dionysiac energy is undertaken by a host of goat-like satyrs, natural Dionysiac creatures 'living ineradicably behind all civilisation', and it is made possible by the particular relationship between the tragic chorus and its Greek audience (1993: 39). In its most rudimentary form, the tragic chorus annuls the audience's sense of itself and enables it imaginatively to overcome the gulfs of state and society that separate its members from one another, reminding it again of an 'overwhelming sense of unity that goes back to the very heart of nature'. This is the metaphysical consolation provided by all tragedy: the sense that life as a Dionysiac force is ultimately 'indestructible, powerful and joyous' whatever the contingent effects on social and political life (p. 39). Tragedy displays a truth about the power of life that gives each individual the will to live expansively and to overcome its own circumstances. In the tragic experience, Nietzsche concludes, man is 'saved by art, and through art life has saved man for itself'.

However, tragedy can only offer man this metaphysical consolation because it represents an Apollonian mediation of Dionysiac force. Experienced on its own terms, the 'ecstasy' of the Dionysiac state lends man such a profound insight into the primal 'essence of things' that he is repelled by the mundanity of everyday life and can no longer function in society (1993: 39). Dionysiac knowledge kills action, which requires a 'veil of illusion'. This illusion is produced by the spatial arrangement of the Greek tragic performance in which 'there was no fundamental opposition between the audience and the chorus: for everything was simply a great, sublime chorus of dancing, singing satyrs, or of those whom the satyrs represented' (p. 41). The loss of any absolute division between chorus and audience enabled the audience imaginatively to project itself into the Dionysiac mass while retaining a certain critical distance from its frenzy. Consequently the performers are both inside and outside the performance, both viewer and viewed, and this doubled position creates 'an image of Dionysiac man for his own contemplation' (p. 42). The satyr chorus is therefore both spontaneous and self-conscious in its movement. In this double movement, Nietzsche argues, lie the beginnings of Greek *drama*: one sees oneself transformed and acting as if one were someone else. The Dionysiac reveller envisages himself as a satyr; it is as a satyr that he gazes upon Dionysius; and the drama is completed in his new vision of a life 'outside himself' which constitutes 'the Apolline complement of his state' (p. 43). From this perspective Nietzsche can characterise Greek tragedy as 'the Dionysiac chorus, continually discharging itself into an Apolline world of images' and drama as the 'Apolline symbol of Dionysiac knowledge' (pp. 43–4).

The tragic chorus presents, then, a shattering insight into the Dionysiac condition of eternal and primal suffering that is 'the sole foundation of the world'. But it also provides images and narratives by which this knowledge can be redeemed and transformed into a basis for life (1993: 25). Nietzsche underlines the interdependence of Dionysiac force and Apollonian form at the conclusion of *The Birth of Tragedy*:

Music and tragic myth are to an equal extent expressions of the Dionysiac capacity of a people, and they are inseparable. Both originate in a sphere of art beyond the Apolline. Both transfigure a region in whose chords of delight dissonance as well as the terrible image of the world charmingly fade away; they both play with the sting of displeasure, trusting to their extremely powerful magical arts; both use this play to justify the existence even of the 'worst world'. Here the Dionysiac, as against the Apolline, proves to be the eternal and original artistic force, calling the whole phenomenal world into existence: in the midst of it a new transfiguring illusion is required if the animated world of individuation is to be kept alive. If we could imagine dissonance becoming man – and what else is a man? – then in order to stay alive that dissonance would need a wonderful illusion, covering its own being with a veil of beauty. This is the real artistic intention of Apollo, in whose name we bring together all those innumerable illusions of the beauty of appearance, which at each moment make life worth living and urge us to experience the next moment.

(1993: 117)

THE DEATH OF TRAGEDY

The aesthetic and ethical power of the Greek tragic vision is constituted by the 'reciprocal necessity' of the Apollonian world of beauty and individuated form and its Dionysiac 'substratum' (1993: 25). By the same token, the decline of Greek tragedy was caused by the *separation* of Apollo and Dionysius. Nietzsche observes three stages in this decline, which he identifies with Euripides, Socrates and Sophocles. None of these figures is ever completely condemned by Nietzsche, because every negation of life retains traces of the energy it represses. In the transition to Sophoclean tragedy, however, Nietzsche identifies a tendency to weakness and morality that is relevant to our modern subjection to outmoded values. The playwright Euripides (484–406 BC) is one of the principal villains of *The Birth of Tragedy* because he inaugurated a series of formal changes in Greek drama that had, Nietzsche argues, profoundly damaging political consequences. His real crime was to have 'abandoned Dionysius' by subordinating Dionysiac myth to a weakened tragic vision solely dependent upon the individuated figure of the dramatic spectator who is brought on stage to represent 'everyday man' (p. 55). This attenuated Euripidean version of tragedy led eventually, Nietzsche argues, to a new mode known as the 'New Attic Comedy', which combined social realism and moral commentary. Instead of the metaphysical or inhuman consolation of tragedy Euripides presented the life and aspirations of the common citizen coupled with a moral appeal to everyday bourgeois self-advancement. Tragedy no longer depicts a competition of forces and drives; now its antagonistic energies are organised from the perspective of the dramatic spectator, whose humours and prejudices are represented on stage by the stock figure of 'everyday man'. The world of tragedy is turned upside-down: now, Nietzsche complains, we see life represented and *judged* by the mediocre and weak. The common man of Euripidean tragedy and the New Comedy has lost interest in an ideal past and an ideal future: he 'values nothing, past or future, more highly than the present' (p. 56). Euripides' 'excision of the primitive and powerful Dionysiac element from tragedy, and the re-building of tragedy on non-Dionysiac art, morality and philosophy' privileged social realism and commentary over the enigmatic depths of the choric mysteries (p. 59). And even though at the end of his life Euripides came to regret hounding Dionysius from the stage, the victory of rationalism and moral critique had already been accomplished by the appearance of one of tragedy's great opponents: Socrates.

The decisive conflict in the narrative of Greek tragedy is staged between Dionysiac myth and Socratic philosophy. This battle 'was to be the downfall of Greek tragedy' (1993: 60). The central problem of Euripidean tragedy, for Nietzsche, was two-fold: it sought its tragic dynamic in the conflict of 'cool, paradoxical *thoughts*', rather than the ordered form of Apollonian art; and it looked merely to evoke an emotional response from its audience rather than remind them of the ecstatic state of Dionysius that persists behind every social structure. Consequently Euripidean tragedy became a form in which *neither* Apollonian nor Dionysiac tragic effects were possible. It found itself 'incapable of achieving the Apolline effect of the epic, and has also made the greatest possible break with the Dionysiac elements, and now, in order to have any effect at all, it needs new stimuli which can no longer be found within either of these aesthetic impulses, neither the Apolline nor the Dionysiac' (p. 61). These stimuli appeared in the teaching of Socrates. Socratic philosophy developed a form of dialogue or 'dialectic' in which competing definitions of moral, political and aesthetic value were examined in a quest for universal truth. With the arrival of Socrates *consciousness*, rather than myth, became the creative principle behind Greek culture. Now philosophy overpowers art, which is increasingly re-modelled according to the progressive logical development of the dialectic. It is, Nietzsche contends, in the three 'optimistic formulae' of Socratic philosophy – virtue is knowledge, all sins come from ignorance, and the virtuous man is the happy man – that we find the 'death of tragedy' (p. 69). Its guiding principle is no longer the

DIALECTIC

In Plato's dialogues, dialectic is a method used by Socrates to arrive at the true Idea or form. Socrates asks various participants in the dialogue for a definition of, say, truth, friendship, justice, beauty or love. He then explores various definitions, finding them partial, inadequate or contradictory. By rejecting all these common opinions and assertions, Socrates' dialectic suggests that the *true* meaning of these ideas needs to be sought beyond mere opinion. The dialectic is negative because it begins by *rejecting*, or being other than, the skilful definitions offered to Socrates by the supposedly clever rhetoricians.

For the German philosopher Georg Wilhelm Friedrich Hegel (1770–1831), the dialectic also takes the form of *negation*. For example, we understand truth to be what we perceive with our senses. But we also understand 'truth' to be what remains the same or is valid for all time. Both senses seem required by the concept of truth, but each sense contradicts the other. Hegel insists that all philosophical concepts have this contradictory, negative or dialectical form. From the contradiction or negation of concepts, Hegel wants to prove that *life* is not immediate. There is no such thing as pure, uncontradictory or positive being. All life is dialectical, involving self-contradiction or negation. In opposition to this negative or dialectical view of life – a view that focuses on concepts and the way in which we think of the world and arrive at truth – Nietzsche insists on a positive or anti-dialectical struggle of life. Here, forces struggle and are different from each other; but there is no *contradiction*. Whereas dialectic moves from contradiction to a higher truth that resolves antagonism, Nietzsche wants to sustain conflict and dynamism without resolution and without any term being the *negation* of the other.

metaphysical consolation that 'beneath the whirlpool of phenomena eternal life flows indestructibly onwards', but rather an aesthetic Socratism in which intelligibility, rather than beauty, defines the nature of tragic vision (p. 75).

The disintegration of Greek tragic art continued with the playwright Sophocles. It manifested itself in Sophocles' attack on the tragic chorus, which seemed to him dispensable 'although we have understood that the chorus can only be seen as the cause of tragedy, and the tragic'

(1993: 70). The role of the chorus is now restricted to the level of an actor; in the process, its essence is destroyed and the seeds of its annihilation sown. From this point it is no longer 'a visual symbolisation of music, the dream world of a Dionysiac rapture' (p. 70). In post-Sophoclean drama the defining role of critical reason is underlined in a new emphasis upon character portrayal, psychological development and dramatic naturalism, while the choric function is reassigned to a number of minor characters. This reconfiguration of tragic art, Nietzsche insists, was the aesthetic complement of a burgeoning Socratic and 'Alexandrian' culture with its democratic reversal of noble values, and shallow belief in the triumphant progress of enlightened 'man'.

Nietzsche's account of the death of Greek tragedy concludes with the elevation of a new life-form called 'theoretical' man. Socratic thought is presented as the precursor to a radically different and anti-tragic culture in which mythic knowledge is deemed to be no knowledge at all. For Socrates, tragedy was 'utterly irrational, full of causes without apparent effects, effects without apparent cause' (1993: 67). It is agreeable without being useful: from this perspective the aesthetic is seen as a diversion from properly moral knowledge, which is synonymous with philosophical and scientific inquiry. The proper task for the man of culture was now to mobilise concepts, arguments and conclusions in order to determine a universal form of knowledge. Socrates is therefore the 'turning point' of world history because his legacy was the construction of 'a common network of rational thought across the globe, providing glimpses of the lawfulness of an entire solar system' (p. 73).

THEORETICAL MAN

Nietzsche's portrait of modern theoretical man offers a melancholy conclusion to his history of tragic art. But in a brilliant twist he also presents Socrates as an *ambivalent* figure whose anti-tragic teaching led, paradoxically, to a renewed desire for tragic knowledge. The irony of Socrates' position is that his belief that rational knowledge could encompass and explain the entire phenomenal world is a benevolent *myth* designed to obscure the limitations of scientific thought. The inevitable failure of science to account for the entire mystery of existence only deepens this irony, for theoretical man is then compelled to appeal once more to the very forces – art and religion – that his rationalism had systematically repressed. The first edition of *The Birth of Tragedy* concludes at this point where the 'insatiable, optimistic zest for knowledge' transforms itself into tragic resignation and a renewed demand for art:

> But now, spurred on by its powerful illusion, science is rushing irresistibly to its limits, where the optimism essential to logic collapses. For the periphery of the circle of science has an infinite number of points, and while it is as yet impossible to tell how the circle could ever be fully measured, the noble, gifted, man even before reaching the mid-course of his life, inevitably reaches that peripheral boundary, where he finds himself staring into the inevitable. If he sees here, to his dismay, how logic twists around itself and finally, bites itself in the tail, there dawns a new form of knowledge, which needs art as both protection and remedy, if we are to bear it.

> (1993: 74–5)

But what shape would this new form of knowledge take and when would it appear? Nietzsche's revised and expanded edition of *The Birth of Tragedy* suggested that a new form of tragic knowledge was being born within modernity in the guise of the 'gradual awakening of the Dionysiac spirit in our contemporary world', represented by German music in its development from Johann Sebastian Bach (1685–1750) and Ludwig van Beethoven (1770–1827) to Wagner (1993: 94). German music is, then, a modern antidote to modernity's investment in the sterile inheritance of Enlightenment rationalism. Nietzsche's analysis of the relation between Greek culture and modern German music, while notable for its celebration of Wagner, is more generally significant as an example of both his strategic use of the past to make a form of life possible in the present and as a diagnosis of the malaise of modernity. He had no merely antiquarian interest in the classical heritage: Greek culture was valuable because it offered a conceptual model for the way we should live *now*. 'For the Greek model is of inestimable value to us', he explained, 'as we stand at the boundary between two different modes of existence; all transitions and struggles assume classical and instructive form in that model' (p. 95). The decline of Greek culture teaches us that without myth 'all culture loses its healthy and natural creative power' (p. 109). This is a crucial lesson, Nietzsche argues, because modern culture has lost its mythic dimension, and without myth humanity has no sense of cultural order and coherence:

> And here stands man, stripped of myth, eternally starving, in the midst of all past ages, digging and scrabbling for roots, even if he must dig for them in the most remote antiquities. What is indicated by the great historical need of unsatisfied modern culture, clutching about for countless other cultures, with its consuming desire for knowledge, if not the loss of myth, the loss of the mythical home, the mythical womb?
>
> (1993: 110)

The crucial role of art within modern culture is to reproduce the example of the Greeks in devising mythic structures that give form to experience while rediscovering the 'true metaphysical meaning of life' (1993: 111). This aesthetic function is fulfilled in poems such as Samuel Taylor Coleridge's 'Kubla Khan' (1797), which returns to the duality of Apollo and Dionysius. The poem begins with Kubla's imposition of order upon chaos:

> In Xanadu did Kubla Khan
> A stately pleasure dome decree:
> Where Alph, the sacred river, ran
> Through caverns measureless to man
> Down to a sunless sea.
>
> (1963: 167)

A region of 'fertile ground' is now 'girded round' with 'walls and towers'. Form and coherence are therefore given to the uncharted and 'measureless' space of nature. This division between form and formlessness helps to constitute the value of human culture: the dome is 'stately' and a place of 'pleasure', not toil or struggle. However, a cultured and Apollonian form divorced from the primal force of Dionysiac existence is in danger of petrifying into a hollow and empty structure. The second stanza of 'Kubla Khan' depicts the persistence of primal and pre-cultural forces as the 'savage place' of nature resists its enclosure within man-made structures:

> But oh! that deep romantic chasm which slanted
> Down the green hill athwart a cedarn cover!
> A savage place! as holy and enchanted
> As e'er beneath a waning moon was haunted

By woman wailing for her demon lover!
And from this chasm, with ceaseless turmoil seething,
As if this earth in fast thick pants were breathing,
A mighty fountain momently was forced:
Amid whose swift half-intermitted burst
Huge fragments vaulted like rebounding hail,
Or chaffy grain beneath the thresher's flail:
And 'mid these dancing rocks at once and ever
It flung up momently the sacred river.

The 'mighty fountain' erupts from the earth, scattering 'huge fragments' of rocks and endangering the stately designs of human culture
and artifice. But as Nietzsche points out, without the mediation of
Apollonian form Dionysiac energy remains merely formless and
chaotic. The role of art is to structure this energy while preserving the
memory of the primal and amoral force of nature. The mediation of
the Dionysiac by the Apollonian is symbolised in 'Kubla Khan' by the
'mingled measure' of the sacred river. The sacred river represents
the aesthetic transformation of pre-cultural energy into a form that
reconnects humanity with the power of the natural world. Its 'mazy
motion' alerts Kubla to the structures required to contain and harness
the inhuman force of nature. In the following lines, the pleasure-dome
is transformed into an aesthetic reflection of the sacral ordering of
nature; that is why the shadow of Kubla's dome of pleasure is cast
upon its waters:

Five miles meandering with a mazy motion
Through wood and dale the sacred river ran,
Then reached the caverns measureless to man,
And sank in tumult to a lifeless ocean:
And 'midst this tumult Kubla heard from far
Ancestral voices prophesying war!
The shadow of the dome of pleasure
Floated midway on the waves;
Where was heard the mingled measure
From the fountain and the caves.
It was a miracle of rare device,
A sunny pleasure-dome with caves of ice!

When Nietzsche reissued *The Birth of Tragedy* fourteen years later in 1886 he appended a new preface entitled 'Attempt at a Self-Criticism', which presents a very different view of the book's central thesis. He restates here his main argument that the Greek craving for 'the image of everything terrible, evil, cryptic, destructive, and deadly underlying existence' arose from a profound desire to experience the fullness of life, and he presents the optimism of scientific ideas and political democracy as a symptom of waning power and psychological fatigue (1993: 6–7). However, he turned against his former romantic belief in a 'nature' prior to, and descriptive of, an ideal aesthetic order. The 'Attempt' is remarkable for its assault upon *The Birth of Tragedy*, which is now characterised as an 'arrogant and fanatical' book (p. 5). Nietzsche mounts this attack because he no longer believes in a distinction between the phenomenal world of everyday life and an eternal and redemptive sphere of value behind appearances. Now all life is seen to be 'based on appearance, art, deception, point of view, the necessity of perspective and error' (p. 8). We should abandon all belief in 'metaphysical consolation' and feel joy in the power and abundance of experience. To achieve this aim we also require a new language capable of exploring the relation between representation, perspective and value. He began to develop this new language in his work on metaphor, and it is to this question that we turn in the next chapter.

SUMMARY

Nietzsche's reading of tragedy offers a radical rereading of Greek art in the service of a non-moral reading of life. It argues that Greek tragedy did not originate in a concept or metaphysical idea, but staged an encounter of material forces that realigned Greek culture with the primal creative force of Dionysius. The triumph of Greek culture was to find a series of Apollonian forms to mediate the destructive force of Dionysiac energy. The demise of Greek culture appears with the uncoupling of Apollo and Dionysius and the elevation of Apollonian conceptual reason in the form of Socratic philosophy. Now concepts like truth, morality and reason are raised above life in order to regulate and judge life. This separation of mankind from the creative power of Dionysius led to a restriction of the manifold force of life within concepts, a restriction that continues to haunt modern existence.

2

METAPHOR

In this chapter we will be looking at Nietzsche's analysis of the origin and constitution of truth. The suggestion that truth might have an 'origin' and 'constitution' may seem puzzling to many readers. After all, we commonly assume that 'truth' represents a timeless and unchanging criterion of assessment by which we establish a proper relationship between thought and experience. Moreover, the propriety of philosophy is usually thought to depend upon a distinction between *values* (which describe the concepts a culture employs to regulate itself, and which vary in different times and places) and *truth* (a transcendent concept that establishes a universal and objective relationship between facts). One of the principal challenges of Nietzsche's work consists in his refutation of this distinction between truth and value. Truth, he argues, does not exist in a transcendent realm beyond the contingency of human values; truth is *itself* a value with a *history* that must be interrogated.

Nietzsche developed his critique of the historical constitution of truth by redefining the relation between truth and *metaphor*. At first glance, these terms might appear to have little in common. We habitually employ the term 'truth' to denote an objective and value-free statement of fact about the world. Something is said to be 'true' if it offers a consistent and unchanging perspective upon the world, irrespective of fluctuations in social and historical circumstance. It is in this sense that we speak of the 'truths' of mathematics and the natural sciences. How-ever, metaphor seems to offer insights of a very different kind. When Shakespeare writes in *The Merchant of Venice* (1598) 'How sweet the moonlight *sleeps* upon this bank' he uses a poetic figure (sleeps) to describe a *literal* or real-world experience (the perception of moonlight reflected upon the earth). This figure is the *metaphorical* term; it presents a new way of perceiving the literal term or subject. Moonlight does not sleep – it has no corporeal life of its own – but by personifying it in this way Shakespeare evokes a human ease and restfulness with which his audience can identify. Metaphorical language clearly has a *relation* to 'objective' and 'factual' descriptions of experience – Shakespeare is providing a vivid and dramatic image to represent the truth of an experi-ence we find everywhere around us – but this representation functions by creating a perspective *upon* the world that does not exist *in* the world. For this reason, the relation between literal and figurative usage is often considered to be a relation between a *stronger* and *weaker* form of truth. The literal becomes synonymous with objectivity and fact – we have all experienced moonlight – while the metaphorical occupies a subordinate role as a figurative representation *of* the truth from a subjective point of view.

   Nietzsche's work relentlessly undermines the elevation of 'literal' over 'metaphorical' truth. He argues that we cannot privilege literal or 'pure' truth over metaphor because truth is *itself* a metaphor that has been invented to lend authority to particular forms of thought and styles of living. He argues repeatedly, for example, that the 'truths' of reli-gious teaching are really dominant *perspectives* upon the meaning of human experience employed to establish the prestige of a community's way of life. However, Nietzsche simultaneously broadens his argument by claiming that *all* of the concepts we employ to represent the 'true' structure of the world – such as 'space', 'time', 'identity', 'causality' and 'number' – are metaphors we project on to the world to make it thinkable in human terms. What we call 'pure' truth is produced by the interchange of poetic figures – 'concepts' – whose origin in *metaphor* has been forgotten. For Nietzsche, the recognition that 'truth' is a figure or perspective we have created in order to represent the world means that we should rethink its function and purpose. His philosophy does not concern itself with providing an objective model of 'the' truth; instead it examines the *history* and *value* of truth as a concept employed to regu-late the manifold force of life.

NON-MORAL THOUGHT

Nietzsche's most concentrated critique of the history and value of truth appears in his essay 'On Truth and Lying in a Non-Moral Sense' (1873), which will be considered in detail below. However, the term 'non-moral' is apt to appear confusing unless it is placed within the broader context of Nietzsche's work. From *The Birth of Tragedy* onwards, Nietzsche consistently argued that both classical and modern cultures were weakened by their dogmatic belief that life and thought should conform to certain abstract and absolute ideas of value. This dogmatic error was inaugurated by Socrates, whose insistence that life be reinterpreted according to universal ideas of truth precipitated the collapse of Greek intellectual culture. Socrates' error was compounded by his disciple, the philosopher Plato, who created a realm of transcendent and eternal 'Ideas' such as 'justice,' 'beauty' and 'the good' which gave all life form. The 'most dangerous of all errors hitherto had been a dogmatist's error,' Nietzsche explains in *Beyond Good and Evil*, 'namely Plato's invention of pure spirit and the good in itself' (1990a: 32). To speak of truth in the Platonic sense as an absolute value before and beyond life – an ideal principle of truth that was not itself merely one more subjective evaluation of the world – is, Nietzsche argues, to mistake its meaning. Truth does not exist as an ideal beyond the multiplicity of perspectives on life; truth is *produced* by these perspectives as a way of establishing the coherence and authority of a particular style of life. Thus in one of his many reflections upon western religious morality in *On the Genealogy of Morality*, first published in German in 1887, Nietzsche argues that the 'truth' of a transcendental world-to-come that will redeem earthly experience was the particular invention of a powerless caste – the Jews – in a bid to gain power over their oppressors. Far from being an ideal and timeless truth, Judaeo-Christian morality establishes a specific perspective upon experience that confers supreme value on human traits – meekness, submissiveness, the renunciation of sensuality and worldly ambition – that were formerly deemed worthless (2000: 31). An alteration in perspective *creates* a new form of truth: what was once judged weak is now the index of all strength. To deny the perspectival nature of truth is to mistake the way in which values emerge. 'To be sure,' Nietzsche explains, 'to speak of spirit and the good as Plato did meant standing truth on her head and denying *perspective* itself, the basic condition of all life' (1990a: 32). It is this

fateful inversion of the relationship between life and truth that is repro-
duced in our own culture by the Christian elevation of a redemptive
moral code above the world of fallen humanity. Christianity, Nietzsche
concludes, is merely 'Platonism for "the people"'; it is a decadent reinterpretation of life through which life loses the creative will to renew
itself.

PLATONIC IDEAS

According to Plato, only Ideas have true being. The sensible world we
experience is always changing and therefore cannot be known. We can only
know what remains the same and what is true eternally. The Ideas are the
eternal, true and otherworldly forms which give the changing sensible world
its relatively knowable shape and constancy. For Plato the sensible world
has no true being; it is a mere copy or semblance of the true world of forms.
The beautiful things we experience, for example, are only *relatively* beautiful
because they participate in, or resemble, the Idea of beauty. The just actions
we see in the world 'have' the quality of justice only because they resemble
the eternal and unchanging idea of justice. For Plato, then, this world is a
secondary world devoid of truth and real being. Only the external world of
Ideas has true being; and the only worthy life focuses on the truths of this
higher world, and not on the flux of experience.

TRUTH AND UNTRUTH

One of the most striking ways in which Nietzsche conceived of his work
was as a 'Prelude to a Philosophy of the Future'. In order to imagine a
future for thought, he claimed, it was necessary to think *beyond* the
Platonic-Christian reinterpretation of life according to a moral idea of
truth. He began this task by posing a series of challenges to the vision
of truth as a grounding moral ideal. Where, he asks in *Beyond Good and
Evil*, first published in German in 1886, does our idea of truth come
from? Is truth really a neutral and disinterested description of the world?
Is it actually possible to separate truth from value? More radically still,
what is it in us that wants truth in the first place?

> What really is it in us that wants the truth? – We did indeed pause for a long
> time before the question of the origin of this will – until finally we came to a

complete halt before an even more fundamental question. We asked after the value of this will. Granted we want truth: why not rather untruth? And uncertainty? Even ignorance? – The problem of the value of truth stepped before us – or was it we who stepped before this problem?

(1990a: 33)

Much of Nietzsche's philosophy may be described as the attempt to find solutions to the problem of the value of truth. His first move is to argue that the 'timeless' ideal of pure disinterested truth has a historical origin in the philosophical *faith in antithetical values* (1990a: 34). Philosophical or 'metaphysical' thought functions, Nietzsche claims, by creating a number of binary oppositions between values like the true, the genuine and the selfless on the one hand and the will to deception, the counterfeit and the will to selfishness on the other. The idea of 'truth' is born when the first term in these oppositions is privileged at the expense of the second. We commonly assume that the 'true', the 'good' and the 'genuine' describe pure and foundational values, whilst what is 'false', 'evil' and 'counterfeit' denotes a secondary *corruption* of these original ideals. However, Nietzsche argues that this view mistakes the way in which our values are created. Far from truth being a foundation against which we can define falsity, the division between truth and falsehood is created by valuations. By referring to a valuation as true, philosophers create the illusion that there are oppositions that *precede* judgement. But the difference between truth and falsehood is an effect of a judgement too weak to admit that it is just one more point of view among others. We use the term 'fiction' – with its associations of artifice, mutability of meaning and manipulation of perspective – routinely to describe a view of experience that lacks the objectivity of pure truth. The effect of this contrast is to *create* an idea of 'truth' as disinterested, universally applicable and perfectly consistent with itself. 'Truth' becomes an ideal standard of value that supposedly exists above and beyond any *particular* perspective upon experience. Fiction, then, is not a corruption of truth: instead, the concept of 'pure' truth is a supreme fiction intended to exalt the idea of absolute and transcendent measure and the moral vision of life. Our ideas of truth and fiction spring from a common origin: it is even possible, Nietzsche notes mischievously, that the value of the true, the genuine and the selfless cannot be separated from appearance, the will to deception and selfishness, but 'resides precisely in their being artfully related and crocheted to these wicked, apparently antithetical things, perhaps even in their being essentially identical with them.' He develops this point in a remarkable passage that argues that fiction and 'untruth' may not only be crucial to the constitution of truth but also fundamental to the advancement of life:

> The falseness of a judgement is to us not necessarily an objection to a judgement: it is here that our new language perhaps sounds strangest. The question is to what extent it is life-advancing, life-preserving, species-preserving, perhaps even species-breeding; and our fundamental tendency is to assert that the falsest judgements (to which synthetic judgements *a priori* belong) are the most indispensable to us, that without granting as true the fictions of logic, without measuring reality against the purely invented world of the unconditional and self-identical, without a continuous falsification of the world by means of numbers, mankind could not live – that to renounce false judgements would be to renounce life, would be to deny life. To recognise untruth as a condition of life: that, to be sure, means to resist customary value-sentiments in a dangerous fashion; and a philosophy which ventures to do so places itself, by that act alone, beyond good and evil.

(1990a: 35–6)

This passage reprises several key Nietzschean themes. Perhaps the most striking claim is Nietzsche's assertion that a judgement may be false but still remain *valuable* to us. The ultimate 'truth' of a judgement, he argues, does not consist in its degree of logical consistency but whether or not it establishes conditions that permit a powerful form of life to develop. What Nietzsche calls the 'will to truth' is not synonymous with an appeal to 'pure' or disinterested knowledge; it expresses itself most profoundly in the drive to create a view of the world that extends and transforms life. The goal of thought is not, therefore, a disinterested idea of 'truth' but the creation of a perspective upon life in which my potential may be realised, my desires satisfied, and my creative instincts fully expressed. Nietzsche happily concedes that such a perspective constitutes a 'false judgement' insofar as it represents a motivated and creative interpretation of life. But what he calls the 'continual falsification of the world' is *indispensable*, rather than hostile, to the constitution of truth because it supplies the 'fictions of logic' that enable humanity to establish the 'truth' of its experience. Life would be strictly *unthinkable* without conceptual fictions such as 'time', 'space' and 'identity' which we impose upon the world; it is only by mobilising these 'false' perspectives that 'thought' can reflect upon the 'meaning' of 'experience'.

The problem confronting thought is *not* that perspectives create truth – this, Nietzsche will demonstrate, is intrinsic to the formation of concepts in general – but that we forget that we have created the truths we employ. Once the perspectival origin of truth is forgotten, Nietzsche continues, these truths ossify into absolute dogmatic beliefs. Nietzsche offers an example of the ossification of perspective into dogma in his reflection upon the Stoic vision of nature:

> You want to live 'according to nature'? O you noble Stoics, what fraudulent words! Think of a being such as nature is, prodigal beyond measure, indifferent beyond measure, without aims or intentions, without mercy or justice, at once fruitful and barren and uncertain; think of indifference itself as a power – how *could* you live according to such indifference? To live – is that not precisely wanting to be other than this nature? Is living not valuating, preferring, being unjust, being limited, wanting to be different? And even if your imperative 'live according to nature' meant at bottom the same thing as 'live according to life' – how could you *not* do that?

(1990a: 39)

Nature, as Nietzsche explained in *The Birth of Tragedy*, is an amoral force of creation and destruction. It is indifferent to mercy, justice and every other moral idea humanity creates to give value to life. The Stoic philosophers renounced the vanity of worldly ambition by appealing instead to the 'truth' of nature, but their version of nature is really a polite philosophical fiction calculated to provide an endorsement of their own mode of life. In Nietzsche's view the Stoic appeal to 'nature' is absurd on two grounds: it is impossible, after all, for 'man' as a natural being to not live 'according to nature' at a certain level; but at the same time the destructive power of nature threatens to destroy every stable interpretation we impose upon the world. The 'truth' of the Stoic position is really quite different: they wanted to create an idea of nature that would make all life exist 'after their own image' (1990a: 39). This benign, moral and *false* vision of natural innocence subsequently hardens into a dogmatic representation; it is resurrected, Nietzsche notes, in every form of romanticism. Indeed, such dogmatism is one of the primary ways in which systems of thought preserve themselves; philosophy, in this sense, is not disinterested knowledge but the 'tyrannical

THE STOICS

Stoicism was one of the new philosophical movements of the Hellenistic period; it also made a major contribution to the intellectual culture of imperial Rome. Some of the principal Stoic thinkers were the Greeks Zeno of Citium (344–262 BC) and Chrysippus (d. c. 206 BC) and the Romans Seneca (4 BC–AD 65), Epictetus (c. 55–135) and the emperor Marcus Aurelius (121–80). The name derives from the 'porch' (*stoa Poikile*) where the members of the group gathered to receive instruction. The Stoics believed that the path to happiness lay in the cultivation of moral and intellectual virtue. Such virtue could only be achieved by the rejection of 'vices' like extreme emotion and worldly ambition, and by developing a serene indifference to the tribulations of fortune. The essence of living well is to recognise the difference between those things that are within or beyond our control and to accept with equanimity the unfolding of our destiny. To live virtuously by renouncing passionate attachment and desire is to live in accordance with the rational order of nature, which embodies in turn the *logos* or reason of God. Stoic virtue therefore commits its adherents to a form of pantheism by perceiving the moral principle of divinity everywhere in the natural world.

drive itself, the most spiritual will to power, to "creation of the world", *prima causa*' (p. 39). For thought to have a future beyond dogmatic ideas, however, it is necessary to recognise untruth as a *condition* of life and create new truths that enable us to organise our drives and abilities in the most productive form. A philosophy conceived in such a way would place itself *beyond* 'good' and 'evil' because it actively created truth without recourse to traditional moral values.

THE ORIGIN OF TRUTH

In 'On Truth and Lying in a Non-Moral Sense' Nietzsche presents a historical theory of the nature and evolution of human thought. He does so in order to challenge the idea that thought manifests itself as the expression of a 'moral sense' and a 'pure drive towards truth' (1999: 142). Nietzsche begins by arguing that the greatest strengths of the human intellect are discovered in *dissimulation*, not in a capacity for truth or a pure moral sense. Dissimulation, he suggests, is fundamental to the development of society because it is the means by which the weak manage to deceive the strong and maintain their hold on existence. The strong are able to take what they need to subsist by brute force; the weak, however, must devise strategies and contrive favourable appearances to protect themselves and ensure a share of the spoils. As a society develops, these primitive forms of subterfuge become codified in social rituals of patronage and etiquette. So pronounced are the arts of dissimulation in the maintenance and development of human society that the *real* question is how the idea of a pure drive towards truth ever appeared in the first place:

> This art of dissimulation reaches its peak in humankind, where deception, flattery, lying and cheating, speaking behind the backs of others, keeping up appearances, living in borrowed finery, wearing masks, the drapery of convention, play-acting for the benefit of others and oneself – in short, the constant fluttering of human beings around the flame of vanity is so much the rule and the law that there is virtually nothing which defies understanding so much as the fact that an honest and pure drive towards truth should ever have emerged in them.

> (1999: 142)

Nietzsche suggests, instead, that the 'pure' drive towards truth is an *effect* of dissimulation and deception. We have seen that each individual practises dissimulation upon its fellows to preserve itself within society. However, the individual's safety is guaranteed more securely by the establishment of social alliances and undertakings that prevent this society from collapsing back into internecine warfare. This condition is established by the transition from concealment and dissimulation towards a general 'peace treaty' that reduces the potential for violence by establishing a common set of rules and prohibitions. It is in the wake of this 'peace treaty', Nietzsche argues, that something emerges 'which looks like the first step towards the acquisition of that mysterious drive for truth' (1999: 143). For if this treaty is to be recognised and enforced the value of truth must be the same in different times and places. In this way the idea of *universal truth* is born. Nietzsche's point is that this new concept of universal truth does not exist as a transcendental idea before and beyond time; it is a secondary effect of the 'legislation of language', which invents a way of designating things that has 'the same validity and force everywhere'. At the same time, the relation between the legislation of language and the law of truth appears in a new distinction between truth and *lying*. From the moment that the laws of language and the possibility of universal truth appear, lying comes into existence as a mode of improper designation and the liar is excluded from good society. Yet even though the law of truth is *effected* by this distinction, humanity only desires truth in a 'limited sense' (p. 143). It does not possess an absolute moral hatred of dissimulation, since it is *through* dissimulation that society comes into being. Humanity merely condemns the baleful consequences of 'certain species of deception' that threaten its security. In the same way, human beings remain indifferent to knowledge if it brings them no immediate benefit and are 'actively hostile' to truths that might undermine their social practices and hierarchies. The will to truth that characterises social development is therefore a means of self-preservation motivated by pragmatic considerations rather than an abstract and absolute idea of value and propriety.

FORGETTING

Nietzsche extends his analysis of truth and knowledge by arguing that it is only through *forgetfulness* that we maintain our belief in pure truth. His analysis of the conventions of language gradually develops a critique of substance and causality. We act as if 'truth alone had been decisive in the genesis of language' and as though a principle of certainty ordained a perfect correspondence between things and the words used to designate them (1999: 144). Yet this, Nietzsche argues, is to mistake the way language works. There is no ideal and essential connection between the substance of a thing and its designation in language. The German language, for example, describes a tree as masculine and a plant as feminine but the attribution of gender is simply a linguistic convention rather than a disclosure of the 'real' nature of a natural object. The arbitrary relation between words and things is obvious from the fact that different languages uses different words to attribute various properties to the same objects. Language is used in this way to *produce*, rather than merely describe, the meaning of things within particular cultural systems. The productive character of language should not surprise us, he continues, once we acknowledge that words are unable to capture the 'full and adequate expression' of a thing (p. 144). Traditional theories of language presupposed that the pure truth of a 'thing-in-itself' lay behind the appearances of phenomena – the world of natural objects –

and that this truth was expressed by the representations of language. This linguistic model therefore charted a movement from an original cause (the ideal thing-in-itself) to its phenomenal appearance (the world of natural forms) and then to its embodiment in words. Nietzsche challenges this idea by insisting that there is no ideal and transcendent cause *outside* us that determines the order and meaning of appearances. Words are not the pure attribution of an inhuman truth, but secondary copies in images and sounds of 'nervous stimulations' of the body and brain (p. 144). What we call 'language' originates in *two metaphors:* the translation of a nerve stimulus into an image (first metaphor) and the imitation of this image in sound (second metaphor). The bodily origin of sense must be *translated* into these metaphors *before* it can become meaningful. It is at this point that Nietzsche radically reinterprets the relationship between metaphor and truth. Metaphors, he insists, are not secondary expressions of an ideal, inhuman and pre-linguistic reality. Instead, the economy of visual and aural metaphors *produces* the shared reality-effect that we call the 'world', which is then reinterpreted in terms of ideal truth and value.

Linguistic meaning, then, is not the pure identity of a concept with the essence of things. The thing-in-itself emerges 'first as a nervous stimulus, then as an image, and finally as an articulated sound' (1999: 145). Thought works retrospectively to efface the memory of a physiological origin of sense by establishing language as the pure embodiment of truth. The substitution of an origin of *meaning* for the interchange of metaphors is not peculiar to language, Nietzsche declares, but definitive of thought in general. He illustrates this point by shifting his focus from language to the general formation of concepts. Concepts are crucial to us because they are the basic units of thought. However, the entire process of conceptualisation is based on a substitution of the general for the particular case. A word does not become a concept as an ideal form of the unique and particular experience from which it derives but only insofar as it 'must fit countless other, more or less similar cases, i.e. cases which, strictly speaking, are never equivalent, and thus nothing other than non-equivalent cases' (p. 145). A concept *becomes* a concept by establishing a metaphorical identity between different forms. Consider, for example, the concept 'blue'. The statement 'no two shades of blue are exactly alike' depends upon the imposition of a conceptual norm – 'blue' in the ideal sense – to measure any degree of divergence (such as 'royal blue' or 'turquoise'). Like every other concept, the concept 'blue' is formed by 'dropping those individual differences arbitrarily, by forgetting those features that differentiate one thing from another' so that 'blue' now becomes the cause and explanation of different intensities of light. The genesis of conceptualisation, like the genesis of language, is always from a movement of difference or non-equivalent qualities to the indifference of a fixed concept. This movement, Nietzsche claims, is profoundly *anthropomorphic* because nature knows neither form nor concepts. We invest in fixed concepts as human beings because the creation of values like 'reason' and 'honesty' enables us to *project* our needs on to the world. Our thought develops, in fact, by elevating a particular model of *human* knowledge – the world made in our own image – and then repressing our own production of this human norm.

TRUTH AND METAPHOR

Nietzsche's radical questioning of the relation between language and thought leads him to a famous redefinition of truth:

> What, then, is truth? A movable army of metaphors, metonymies, anthropomorphisms, in short a sum of human relations which have been subjected to poetic and rhetorical intensification, translation, and decoration, and which, after they have been in use for a long time, strike a people as firmly established, canonical and binding; truths are illusions of which we have forgotten that they are illusions, metaphors which have become worn by frequent use and have lost all sensual vigour, coins which, having lost their stamp, are now regarded as metal and no longer as coins.
>
> (1999: 146)

Nietzsche's point is *not* that there is no such thing as 'truth', but that we have forgotten – or deliberately repressed – the fact that the concept of truth was willed into existence to reduce social conflict and enable the development of new forms of life. What began as the provisional linguistic and social compromise of a peace-treaty has solidified into an absolute law. Now the law of 'truth' has become an ultimate foundational concept to which all life must conform. Nietzsche argues that the establishment of this law has fundamentally redefined our sense of what it means to be 'human'. Once the law of truth has been established, human beings conceive of themselves as 'human' because of their *potential* for 'truth' and 'reason'. 'As creatures of reason,' he explains, 'human beings now make their actions subject to the rule of abstractions; they no longer tolerate being swept away by sudden impressions and sensuous perceptions; they now generalise all these impressions first, turning them into cooler, less colourful concepts in order to harness the vehicle of their lives and actions to them' (1999: 146). Human beings distinguish themselves from animals by their capacity to accept abstract ideas and to universalise intuitions and perceptions into fixed concepts; we discover the mark of the human in the ability to 'sublimate sensuous metaphors into a schema, in other words, to dissolve an image into a concept'. The purpose of this new conceptual schema is to produce a *system of morality* and a series of *truth-effects*. Nietzsche's history of truth seeks to demonstrate the untruth of the claim that humanity is born with an *innate* moral sense that causes it to develop certain ideas and attitudes to the world. Instead, we are gradually placed under a social obligation to organise perception according to fixed concepts like 'truth' and 'morality'. We experience this obligation as a moral duty, which rigidifies through repetition over time into a moral *truth*.

In modern society, Nietzsche argues, the questions of 'morality' and 'truth' have become almost wholly constitutive of what we take the 'human' to be. This development is reflected in the endless moral injunctions voiced on chat-shows to learn true liberty by becoming 'true to yourself'. What we have forgotten, Nietzsche notes, is that what is meant by truth here is mere adherence to the 'customary metaphors' of social convention (1999: 146). He describes the firmly established conventions of social and moral life as metaphors because the passage of time leads us to forget that these dominant values are nothing more than strong and durable *representations* of the world that have proved successful in promoting certain forms of life (the Christian world view, for example, or the values of the ruling class). Our obliviousness to the historical origins of our values produces an *unconscious* dependence upon shared mores which, because of their familiarity, gradually evolve into new ideals of truth. In this way, the 'truth' of a value is eventually determined by the regularity of its employment: the more frequently a value is evoked, the 'truer' it becomes.

THE SELF

Nietzsche extends his critique of truth and metaphor to the concept of the *self*. One of the major flaws of metaphysical thought, he argues, is that it presupposes an essential substance or 'subject' *behind* appearances that gives appearances their *meaning*. Nietzsche famously recasts this presupposition in linguistic terms by employing a distinction between the 'subject' of a sentence and the 'predicate' (that which affirms or denies something concerning the nature *of* that subject). He challenges the commonplace assumption that 'the subject "I" is the condition of the predicate "think"' (1990a: 47). The problem with this assumption for Nietzsche is that thinking is seen to be an *effect* of a sovereign and independent subject capable of recognising the natural self-evidence of the world imagined as a 'thing in itself'. He objects to this statement because by identifying an 'I' before and behind thought it 'only contains an *interpretation* of the event and does not belong to the event itself'. By 'the event' Nietzsche refers to the multiplicity of sensations, drives and muscular movements that enable a 'self' to express itself in action. Our belief in the idea of a unified subject is contingent, he claims, upon the assumption that a self stands apart from the event of thought and consciously expresses its 'will'. The problem with this belief, however, is that 'will' and 'thinking' are not autonomous and 'higher' levels of being that determine the identity of the self; they are simply *metaphors* for the 'many varieties of feeling' that occupy different roles in the body's physiological economy (1990a: 48). It is hardly surprising that we commonly elide 'willing', 'thinking' and 'action': the conflation of these metaphors permits us to establish the concept of an 'I' upon which all notions of subjective autonomy are based. But 'I', Nietzsche complains, is just a retrospective synthesis of the series of conflicts that bring it into being. An effect and an act of interpretation – the 'I' that wills and acts – has been transformed into the origin of our identity. In this sense, 'free will' is not the ultimate subjective ground of human identity; it is merely the way we view actions after the event. Nietzsche's conviction that 'thinking' and the 'self' are metaphorical effects of physiological drives appears in a remarkable late aphorism:

The 'spirit', something that thinks: where possible even 'absolute, pure spirit' – this conception is a second derivative of that false introspection which believes in 'thinking': first an act is imagined which simply does not occur, 'thinking', and secondly a subject-substratum in which every act of thinking, and nothing else, has its origin: that is to say, both the deed and the doer are fictions.

(1968: 264)

The startling conclusion Nietzsche draws from this assertion is that we generate our beliefs about truth and morality from the grammatical structure of our language rather than from an 'objective' reading of the world. We only believe, that is, in a division between appearance and reality or between essence and expression because our language enforces a distinction between a subject and predicate of thought. The 'real' world is, in fact, a continuous stream of physiological perceptions which we reduce and divide up into concepts such as 'subject', 'object', 'will' and 'origin'. These concepts are an effect of our 'grammatical custom that adds a doer to every deed' (1968: 268). Nietzsche insists that we attend to the formation of substances and identities from this stream of perception because this process is central to the forces of social and political *repression*. A 'self', for Nietzsche, has no metaphysical or substantial identity; it 'is' merely the totality of its actions. However, once the distinction has been made between a set of actions and a substantial self who is *responsible* for those actions it becomes possible to judge individuals in moral terms according to the degree of their adherence to social and political norms. The great emancipatory concept of 'free will' is, in these terms, one of the most repressive inventions imaginable because humanity is now deemed 'free' to reflect upon the need for moral prohibitions and 'guilty' if it chooses to transgress them. In this sense Christian teaching, for which the idea of free will is axiomatic, is a rhetoric of judgement rather than liberation and enshrines a 'hangman's metaphysics' at the core of human affairs (1990b: 65).

ART

Nietzsche relentlessly interrogates the development of conceptual reason because it provides a supposedly universal language within which perceptions and intuitions may be classified and judged in terms of their conformity to a pre-established ideal of truth. Once this 'infinitely complicated cathedral of concepts' has been erected upon the 'moving foundations' of life it also becomes possible to speak of a universal *human nature*, since these laws, distinctions and classifications apply to people in every time and place (1999: 147). Nietzsche objects, however, that this new configuration of thought is profoundly mistaken in its understanding of cause and effect. We should not seek to discover the truth of what it means to be human in universal principles of reason; we should understand that these new conceptual laws *produce* our idea of an essential human nature in the first place. By judging the flux of life according to concepts all we do is translate the world into human terms. It may well be comforting for us to make ourselves the measure of all things, but this anthropomorphic idea of truth is inherently circular because it looks to unriddle the secret of 'man' in a language we invented for ourselves.

Because the law of conceptual reason works tirelessly to establish 'man' as the universal ground of truth, any challenge to this law potentially transforms our idea of what it means to be human. Nietzsche identifies such a radical challenge in art. The power of art is that it continually reminds us of the metaphorical origins of our conceptual systems – that fact that every concept is the 'left-over *residue of a metaphor*' – by attending to the singularity of perception before it is assimilated into an abstract system of values (1999: 147). Art enables us to rethink the formation and self-identity of concepts by offering other ways in which the relation between subjects and objects may be understood. The artist speaks 'in forbidden metaphors and unheard-of combinations of concepts so that, by at least demolishing and deriding the old conceptual barriers, he may do creative justice to the impression made on him by the mighty, present intuition' (p. 152). These remarks are indicative of a powerful strain of Nietzsche's rhetoric that celebrates the artist as a man of culture who gives coherent expression to life. But we must also acknowledge his parallel insistence that the man of reason is *also* a type of artist – although he may not see himself as one – who *produces* a vision of 'reality' by transforming a poetic relation into a conceptual system of values. The difference between these two figures is that the latter is *reactive* in the sense that his art – the art of 'reason' – is designed to ward off, rather than embrace, the multiple possibilities afforded by his creative instincts. This distinction between active and reactive ways of thinking and the conviction that art should be an active *affirmation* of life are crucial entailments of Nietzsche's reflection upon metaphor, which he develops in his later work on morality, will and power.

The power of art to illuminate the metaphorical origins of our dominant ideas about life is the subject of the lyric 'Sunday Morning' by the American poet Wallace Stevens (1879–1955). Stevens's poem reflects upon our investment in the religious distinction between a transcendent world of eternal being and the mundane human world of contingency and change. The poem opens with a woman taking coffee and oranges on a sunlit Sunday morning. The fullness and richness of taste and colour, enjoyed in the warmth and fullness of morning light, affords her a small, sensual moment of transcendence. Her apprehension of the perfection of this moment leads her to reflect upon what such transcendence might mean, and her thoughts drift irresistibly 'Over the seas, to silent Palestine, | Dominion of the blood and sepulchre'. Startled by this almost unconscious passage from the plenitude of sensual pleasure to the divinity of Christian sacrifice, the woman is moved to consider the relation between human and mythic accounts of what is eternal in our nature:

> Why should she give her bounty to the dead?
> What is divinity if it can come
> Only in silent shadows and in dreams?
> Shall she not find in comforts of the sun,
> In pungent fruit, and bright green wings, or else
> In any balm or beauty of the earth.
> Things to be cherished like the thought of heaven?

'Sunday Morning' focuses upon the division that has opened between the worlds of myth and human experience. Too often, Stevens suggests, the contrast between the 'inhuman birth' and 'mythy mind' of the gods and our own fallen existence threatens to overwhelm us. We feel weak and inadequate before the thought of Paradise; the ideas of divinity and transcendence seem only to expose the futility of our human striving. Stevens's poem asks us instead to take courage and remember the *sensual origin* of the idea of divinity. If we do so, the remote indifference and pristine perfection of the concept of Paradise becomes emblematic of our own creative power:

> Shall our blood fail? Or shall it come to be
> The blood of Paradise? And shall the earth
> Seem all of Paradise that we shall know?

> The sky will be much friendlier then than now,
> A part of labor and a part of pain,
> And next in glory to enduring love,
> Not this dividing and indifferent blue.

Rather than perceiving the 'dividing and indifferent blue' of the sky as indicative of the unbridgeable chasm separating us from the divine image of transcendence, 'Sunday Morning' entreats us to open ourselves up to the transcendence of the world we have created for ourselves. The 'blood of Paradise' need *not* be the blood of Christian sacrifice; it could be the expression of our 'labor' and 'pain' in bringing our capacity for creativity and joy to perfection. In Nietzschean terms, nothing divides us from realising our highest nature except the will to accept the challenge. When we do so, we will no longer think about transcendence and 'Paradise', but rather the self-overcoming of our nature in its transition to a higher phase of life. The closing movement of 'Sunday Morning' shares this revaluation of the sensual human world of struggle and self-transformation. In place of an absolute division between the mundane and transcendental worlds, the poem gradually draws these worlds together to show that the 'divine' is constituted by our own imaginative and metaphorical 'weavings'. Divinity is a metaphor we use to express what is most profound and precious in our own nature. Now 'Paradise' is no longer seen as an ideal and timeless value; it is the creation of men and women who must die, dressed in our colours, a lasting testimony to our capacity to sustain and reinvent ourselves:

> Is there no change of death in Paradise?
> Does ripe fruit never fall? Or do the boughs
> Hang always heavy in that perfect sky?
> Unchanging, yet so like our perishing earth,
> With rivers like our own that seek for seas
> They never find, the same receding shores
> That never touch with inarticulate pang?
> . . . Alas, that they should wear our colours there
> The silken weavings of our afternoons,
> And pick the strings of our insipid lutes!
> Death is the mother of beauty, mystical,
> Within whose burning bosom we devise
> Our earthly mothers waiting, sleeplessly.

SUMMARY

Nietzsche rethinks the customary division between truth and metaphor to argue that the idea of pure truth is itself a form of metaphor and a particular perspective upon life. As human thought and culture developed, we forgot that truth originated as a metaphor that allowed us to impose our values and perspectives upon the world, and raised it to the level of an objective and absolute ideal form. The perception that truth is, in fact, an interpretative convention and a dominant perspective upon life means that we should attend both to its history and to the types of value it promotes. To reinforce this perception, Nietzsche presents a history of the non-moral origins of the idea of universal truth in order to show that its belated identification with mankind's innate moral sense lies at the historical origin of our idea of the 'human'. To understand life in terms of its fidelity to abstract and universal concepts is to have a reactive view of the world. Conversely, the artist expresses an active mode of existence by exposing the metaphorical origins of truths and concepts so that we might develop new perspectives upon life.

3

GENEALOGY

In order to understand the development and scope of Nietzsche's work, we need to examine his concepts of 'genealogy' and 'genealogical critique'. Nietzsche developed what he described as a 'genealogical' mode of analysis in order to distinguish his approach from that of traditional historians of morality and culture. His genealogical critique of 'morality' and 'history' will be the focus of this and the following two chapters. As we have seen, Nietzsche's reflection on metaphor explored the historical origin and constitution of our concept of 'truth'. His work on 'genealogy' extends this project in order to consider how we should understand the historical development of our moral values. This project receives its most sustained expression in *On the Genealogy of Morality*. In this book, Nietzsche sets himself both a historical and a methodological problem. The historical question may be stated simply: by what path did we arrive at the 'moral' evaluation of humanity that assumes our highest and best values to be represented by belief in 'Christianity', 'conscience' and modern egalitarian politics? The methodological question poses the problem of how we determine the concept of 'value' in the first place. Is it not true, Nietzsche asks, that we determine our ideas of value on the basis of *prior* values? Does not the entire history of 'morality' *presuppose* both the value of morality and a sovereign individual with a natural capacity for moral responsibility?

Nietzsche's genealogical critique attempts, instead, to trace the emergence of moral values *without* relying upon a prior determination of the value and nature of 'morality' and 'man'. He continually rethinks the relationship between the origin and purpose of a practice or belief to demonstrate that what we call the 'history of morality' represents a collection of authoritative *interpretations* of the development of life. The moral idea of 'man' we know today, Nietzsche conjectures, may in fact be an *ad hoc* development of various historical practices rather than the inevitable outcome of our moral progress. His radicalised vision of history as the successive reinterpretation of the meaning and function of life also compels him to ask two further questions. If the emergence of historical values consists in the movement between authoritative interpretations of life, should we not attend to the *shifts* and *discontinuities* between historical practices rather than searching for a pattern and purpose – such as mankind's innate moral capacity or the Christian narrative of struggle and redemption – that might link these practices together? And if the 'meaning' of history is produced by the conflict *between* these different interpretations, is not the most important task before us to establish an interpretation of the past that enables us to live productively and creatively in the present?

PHILOLOGY

Perhaps the clearest way of introducing Nietzsche's genealogical method is to re-situate his work within the context of nineteenth-century *philology*. The discipline of philology had taken shape in the nineteenth century as a study of the historical emergence of various bodies of knowledge. A philologist inquired into the history of religion, mythologies, the sciences and so on. Nietzsche was trained initially as a philologist, and he took up the chair of classical philology at Basel University in 1869. However, he gradually became disillusioned with what he considered to be the outdated and unphilosophical attitude to the problem of historical value propagated by traditional philology. Nietzsche's attitude becomes clear if we examine the tension within nineteenth-century philology between traditional and modern readings of mythic and historical narratives. Traditional philology was motivated by the attempt to discover from the scattered fragments of archaeological evidence the original identity or event that stood 'behind' a text and gave it its 'meaning'. When conventional biblical scholars examined the archaeological remains of scriptural narratives, for example, they were not concerned primarily with local idiomatic variations or stylistic incongruities; instead, they focused their attention upon what these texts revealed about the original source of spiritual meaning represented by the word of God. Similarly, philological scrutiny of a text such as the *Odyssey* was undertaken to establish immutable facts about the 'mind' and 'genius' of Homer. In both of these examples, the meaning of historical narratives and cultural values was determined by a hermeneutic reference *back* from the constitution of a text to the foundational concept that established its 'identity' and 'truth'.

Nietzsche began as a philologist by inquiring into the origins of cultural and mythological practices, but then transformed the very notion of what our approach to an historical 'origin' might be. Modern philology, as it was extended and practised by Nietzsche, is distinguished by its refusal to accept the hermeneutic reference back from the materiality of a text to the concept and value 'behind' it. His work switches the focus of scholarship from the primordial identity of a concept or value to the *disparate, discontinuous and contingent* forces that create concepts in the first place. It is no longer sufficient, from Nietzsche's perspective, to advance a 'teleological' or end-oriented reading of historical phenomena (a reading that views history as the unfolding of an original purpose towards an ultimate goal); nor is it adequate to interpret cultural forms as if they were merely the expressions of prior ideas or meanings. To 'understand' a cultural artefact such as the Bible we need to take account of a series of unintended and contingent events. Thus, what effect does the order in which biblical texts appear have upon our reading of the past? Who has access to these documents, and what effect does this have upon the way they are interpreted? What significance does the vested interests of scholars – or the rivalries between them – have upon the value that is attached to them? And to what extent is the importance of a text determined by its relationship to broader social and historical forces? In the light of these questions, perhaps the meaning of the Bible and the *Odyssey* consists less in the expression of a mind or vision and more in the struggle for authority between competing interpretations of society, history and morality.

We might underline the distinction between these two approaches to historical practice – traditional hermeneutics of philology versus Nietzsche's suspicion of origins – by turning briefly to the literary genre of the novel. Classic accounts of the development of this genre, such as Ian Watt's *The Rise of The Novel* (1957), describe a two-fold process: a shift in the structure of capitalism leading to a new relationship between the individual and social hierarchies; and the subsequent appearance of a new imaginative form called the 'novel' to explore this transformed relationship. The phrase 'rise of the novel' therefore describes a period in cultural history (roughly the mid-point of the seventeenth-century) when a new imaginative form appeared which opened up new ways of representing human experience. To describe a 'rise' of the novel suggests a moment of meaningful birth, where the novel expresses the discovery of the new category of the 'individual'. On such a reading the novel refers to a coherent and unified event. By contrast, one could see this attempt to historicise the novel by trans-forming it into a singular and self-identical event or category as a refusal of all the competing forces and different styles and genres that emerged. A challenge to this canonical view of 'the novel' as a unified genre has been presented by more recent readings (Davis 1997; Hunter 1990; Stallybrass and White 1986) which present the genre of the novel as a *reduction* of a dynamic series of interchanges between events and prac-tices to the singularity of a fixed concept. Thus what we accept today as a unitary concept with an endless capacity for mutation – in the way we speak variously of the 'realist', 'romantic' and 'postmodern' novel – actually emerges from a mobile and unstable relationship between specific social practices (such as letter-writing and the keeping of diaries), different types of writing (political broadsheets and pamphlets, for example, as well as travel narratives and the multiple registers of the modern newspaper) and the generic norms and constraints imposed by institutional sites like the library and the printing press. In this way, a revisionary and 'genealogical' analysis of the novel exposes the ways concepts are employed to provide an *ex post facto* (retrospec-tive or after the fact) rationalisation of the collection of multiple, *ad hoc* and contingent forces that bring these concepts into being.

CONCEPT AND FORCE

Nietzsche's development of a form of genealogical critique to question particular concepts and values is evident in *The Birth of Tragedy*. His work on tragedy may be distinguished from classical, Renaissance and modern versions of the tragic because he does not conceive of tragedy as a *concept*. There is not one *essence* of tragedy, such as the idea of irresolvable metaphysical and social conflict. The concept of tragedy is usually represented in terms of an essential conceptual division between the mundane world of human striving and a particular ideal of justice and retribution. Tragedy is given a governing idea – the idea of a self or particular set against fate or universality – which is gradually refined throughout its history. We see this concept of tragic conflict variously at work in Sophocles' play *Oedipus the King*, where Oedipus' attempt to restore order in his kingdom of Thebes is thwarted by the malign fate preordained for him by the gods to kill his father and marry his mother. This classical idea of tragedy as a fall provoked by hubris – the over-reaching of an individual who does not respect the limits set by the gods – is then reconfigured in Renaissance culture to explore the limits of individualism in a world gradually moving beyond the fixed hierarchies of feudal social structures. In Shakespeare's *Macbeth* (1605), for example, tragic conflict is relocated within the concept of individual 'virtue'; it finds expression in Macbeth's struggle between the obligation of fealty (his duty as a subject to King Duncan) and the rewards of ambition. By the time we reach a modern tragedy such as Arthur Miller's *Death of a Salesman* (1949), the *concept* of tragic conflict has been adapted for a secular and bourgeois world. 'Tragedy' inheres now supposedly in the conflict between the competing claims of the private world of the family and the public world of work that prevents Willy Lomax from fulfilling his obligations as a husband and father.

For Nietzsche, however, 'tragedy' was *not* a concept nor was it primarily associated with the representation of meaning or values. In contrast to those interpretations of tragedy that progress from an *idea* of tragic conflict to its imaginative representation, Nietzsche's meditation on Greek tragedy remains resolutely at the pre-conceptual level of material political *forces*. The conflict of Greek tragedy was not of ideas – the ideal versus the mundane or the universal versus the particular – but of forces. Gods and men struggled on stage; chorus and characters oscillated with competing voices; ideas and concepts were disrupted by music and gesture. Tragic art, for Nietzsche, does not provide a moral interpretation of life; nor does it offer a teleological vision of a purpose or goal to existence. Instead, the value of tragedy is that it momentarily aligns us with the most profound material force – the endless becoming of life itself – beyond any thought of metaphysical consolation or the hope of redemption. To enter into the tragic experience was to move beyond the narrow confines of the individual and become part of the eternal flux of life in which suffering, pain and violence are inextricably linked to joy, power and creativity. Such experience led the Greeks beyond moral concepts to the material process from which all concepts are born:

> Anyone who approaches these Olympians with a different religion in his heart, seeking elevated morals, even sanctity, ethereal spirituality, charity and mercy, will quickly be forced to turn his back upon them, discouraged and dis-appointed. Nothing here suggests asceticism, spirituality or duty – everything speaks of a rich and triumphant existence, in which everything is deified, whether it be good or evil.
>
> (1993: 21–22)

THE CREATION OF 'MORAL' MAN

Nietzsche's *On the Genealogy of Morality* examines the history and value of moral ideas. These two questions are fundamentally linked for Nietzsche, because if moral values may be seen to have a history it becomes possible to consider whose interests they serve and what vision of life they promote. Moreover, if morality is revealed to be a histor-ical interpretation of life rather than a natural capacity for self-regulation shared by all men and women, we might be able to supplant the *moral* determination of values with another interpretation of our own: an interpretation that does not simply assume – as morality does – that there simply *are* values to be discovered. In *On the Genealogy of Morality* and *Beyond Good and Evil* Nietzsche offers both a critique of the history of morality and a vision of a new 'aristocratic' mode of life beyond moral values. He argues that 'morality' is the triumphant invention of a 'descending' or decadent interpretation of existence. Whereas an 'ascending' or active interpretation of life celebrates the power of a strong will to create and affirm its own values, the moral vision of life establishes transcendental values *above* life – such as the distinction between 'good' and 'evil' – to which all life must conform. Nietzsche's genealogy of values contests this process by exposing the history of morality to be the successive reinterpretation of a set of pre-moral cultural practices. In contrast to earlier moral genealogists who sought merely to refine this history, Nietzsche's purpose is to identify and over-come the values that underpin moral ideas. By demonstrating that 'morality' is a historically specific reinterpretation of the will to power that culminates in a weak and exhausted form of life, he prepares the ground for the non-moral vision of life that characterises his mature work.

Nietzsche's critique of moral thought is sometimes misunderstood because he employs the terms 'master' or 'noble' morality in works such as *Human, All Too Human*, first published in German in 1879, and *On the Genealogy of Morality*, to describe a positive affirmation of life. The key distinction here between 'master morality' and what Nietzsche will characterise as the reactive or 'slave morality' of western thought is that the former *describes* a noble mode of life experienced as the personal, pre-reflective and spontaneous experience of vital being whereas the latter *prescribes* an abstract code of rules and prohibitions that is to be imposed alike upon *every* form of human life. 'Master morality' should be understood, in other words, as the translation into a moral vocabulary of an ascending or powerful mode of being that existed triumphantly before a process of moralisation was invented to reduce humanity to a tame and 'civilised' social animal. Nietzsche marks the passage from the pre-moral 'morality' of noble being to the later conception of morality as a life-denying judgement upon life in a crucial passage from *The AntiChrist*, first published in German in 1894:

> . . . *Morality* no longer the expression of the conditions under which a nation lives and grows, no longer a nation's deepest instinct of life, but become abstract, become the antithesis of life – morality as a fundamental degradation of the imagination, as an 'evil eye' for all things . . .

(1990b: 148)

As this extract demonstrates, 'morality' becomes a problem for Nietzsche when it is transformed from a description of a nation's 'deepest instinct of life' (its values or mores) to an 'abstract' and inflexible law that determines for each individual how life should be lived.

The second essay of the *Genealogy*, 'Bad Conscience', presents a history of what Nietzsche calls the 'moralisation' of 'man' and a more general reflection upon the methodological principles underlying genealogical critique. Here he argues that 'man' makes the transition from a natural to a social animal by means of a form of psychological training designed to 'breed an animal which is able to make promises' (2000: 38). Such training is crucial to the development of social responsibility because our capacity to stand surety for our statements and beliefs depends upon continuity between the commitments we accept and the actions we undertake. The cultivation of responsibility therefore focuses upon the creation of a memory for 'man' so that he understands the connection between a past statement and a present action. Once he recognises the necessary link between 'I shall do' and 'the actual discharge of the will' he has accepted an image of himself as 'reliable, regular, automatic' because his identity is self-consciously understood as continuous and consistent across time (2000: 39).

The perception of an individual with a sufficient sense of responsibility to make and keep a promise is intrinsic, Nietzsche notes, to our idea of 'free will' and the morally autonomous 'sovereign individual' (2000: 40). This individual no longer need conform to the morality of custom – the accumulated burden of traditional law enforced upon a tribe – but becomes morally self-determining and the *standard of his own value* insofar as he decides which course of action is consistent with his own view of the world. This passage from custom to moral self-determination constitutes an epochal shift in the history of the self. It is accompanied by the emergence of a new human faculty – conscience – by which 'man' preserves the memory of his own moral responsibilities:

> The proud realisation of the extraordinary privilege of *responsibility*, the aware-ness of this rare freedom and power over himself and his destiny, has penetrated him to the depths and become an instinct, his dominant instinct: what will he call his dominant instinct, assuming that he needs a word for it? No doubt about the answer: the sovereign man calls it his *conscience* . . .
>
> (2000: 40)

We blithely assume, Nietzsche continues, that 'conscience' and moral self-consciousness represent an innate capacity for moderation and self-regulation which will prevent us from descending into violence, cruelty and barbarism. Nietzsche challenges this naive historical assumption by claiming that our 'natural' moral sense is *produced*, rather than compromised, by a cultural regime of violence and cruelty. Far from being natural capacities, 'memory' and 'conscience' are the belated historical effects of a concerted 'technique of mnemonics' which employs pain and punishment to create a permanent fear of moral transgression:

When man decided he had to make a memory for himself, it never happened without blood, torments and sacrifices: the most horrifying sacrifices and forfeits (the sacrifice of the first-born belongs here), the most disgusting mutilations (for example, castration), the cruellest rituals of all religious cults (and all religions are, at their most fundamental, systems of cruelty) – all this has its origin in that particular instinct which discovered that pain was the most powerful aid to mnemonics.

(2000: 41)

ACTIVE SEPARATION

The opening section of 'Bad Conscience' announces one of Nietzsche's most important themes: the idea of his own 'genealogy' as the *active separation* of different types of value and different levels of being. This difficult theme becomes easier to understand when we recall that 'genealogy' for Nietzsche is both a way of re-examining the history of morality and a way of creating distinctions between 'higher' and 'lower' values. In the first essay in the *Genealogy* on 'Good and Evil' and 'Good and Bad', Nietzsche criticises English psychologists for proposing a history of morality that is *'essentially* unhistorical' (2000: 12). Their errors are revealed, Nietzsche argues, in their discussion of the derivation of the concept and judgement 'good'. The mistake these psychologists made, he suggests, was to detect the origin of the 'good' in selfless and unegoistic acts by the powerful – such as sparing the lives of the weak and allowing them forms of subsistence within society – which were judged good by their *recipients*. In this version of moral history, 'goodness' is a value created by the *weak* to reward the strong for their benevolent restraint and thereby to preserve their fragile and embattled existence. However, as time passed the origin of 'goodness' as a *strategic* celebration of restraint and forbearance was forgotten, and it was gradually transformed into an ideal and timeless standard of *moral* virtue. Good was no longer defined as what was *good for* certain individuals – those who had not been punished – but became an impersonal good *per se*. It becomes good in general to refrain from violence. The values of the weak become universal values.

Nietzsche rebels against this version of moral history for two reasons. As we will see in Chapter 5, he argues that it is impossible for the weak actively to create values; they may *react* against a structure of value that is already in place, but the primary separation of noble from base life is

EMPIRICISM AND PSYCHOLOGY

Empiricism has a long history, stretching back to ancient Greek philosophy, but English empiricism and the tradition of psychology goes back to the Scottish Enlightenment thinker David Hume (1711–76). For Hume, all our supposedly timeless, logical and universal principles – such as causality, necessity, identity and lawfulness – are effects of experience; they are fictions that the mind imposes on experience. Even the self or subject who supposedly precedes and is the ground of experience is, for Hume, a fiction: an assumed identity that allows us to order our world and our selves into manageable and liveable forms. The traditions of psychology and associationism that followed Hume tried to explain the 'laws' of the human mind, mapping all the ways in which the flux of sense experience could be synthesised into a coherent world of cause and effects. Other thinkers, such as the Earl of Shaftesbury (1671–1713), even argued for a moral sense: the good was no longer some external ideal, but human beings had an innate capacity to order and judge the world in terms of virtues and vices, or what is beneficial and harmful to humanity. This tradition of psychologism therefore eliminated timeless and inhuman laws of logic, but then made the human psyche lawful, regular and commonsensical. Against this tradition, Nietzsche's empiricism argues that ideas, identities and laws are fictions imposed by the mind. But he does not see the human mind or psyche as lawful or benevolent. Instead of assuming that there is 'a' human psyche that will always order the world in a regular and causal manner, Nietzsche investigates how general ideas – including the idea of humanity – have been caused. What sort of sense impressions, he asks – such as punishment and images of morality – have produced moral 'man'?

wholly beyond them. He also dissents from this history because it accepts a particular *perspective* upon social practice – the idea of goodness as selfless benevolence proposed by the weak – and refashions it into a template with which to determine moral values *in general*. This error, Nietzsche argues, substitutes a reactive acceptance of moral *norms* for the active creation of moral *values*. Goodness, he continues, does not emanate from those to whom goodness is shown; instead, it is the 'good' themselves – the strong, noble and creative individuals – who first ascribed the value 'good' to their own actions (2000: 12). The strong do so by affirming their own will and actively separating themselves from every weak and base form of life. The creation of values like 'good' and 'bad' is an effect of this active separation of powerful from weak being. Nietzsche refers to this differential movement at the origin of values as the 'pathos of distance' that is enforced between levels of life. 'The pathos of nobility and distance,' he explains, 'the continuing and predominant feeling of complete and fundamental superiority of a higher ruling kind in relation to a lower kind, to those "below" – that is the origin of the antithesis "good" and "bad"' (2000: 13). 'Genealogy', for Nietzche, means an attention both to historical origins and to the movement of separation between active and reactive forms of life that brings our values into being. To quote the French philosopher Gilles Deleuze (1925–95) in his book on Nietzsche's philosophy:

> Genealogy means both the value of origin and the origin of values. Genealogy is as opposed to absolute values as it is to relative or utilitarian ones. Genealogy signifies the differential element of values from which value itself derives. Genealogy thus means origin or birth, but also difference or distance in the origin.
>
> (1983: 2)

BAD CONSCIENCE

Nietzsche's genealogical critique focuses particularly upon the reversal of cause and effect at work when *material* practices like sacrifice and mutilation are used to produce a new form of life – such as the interior subjective space of 'memory' and 'conscience' – that is subsequently identified as the 'natural' ground of moral values. He extends his analysis by reconsidering the origins of 'bad conscience'– or the 'consciousness of guilt' – and punishment. This is one of Nietzsche's most important and controversial arguments, because it asks us to reconsider some of our most basic assumptions about justice, law and retribution. Traditional genealogists of morality, Nietzsche claims, have assumed that punishment is meted out as a response to a form of moral transgression. This assumption is at the basis of both our moral and legal systems. From this perspective, it becomes 'right' to punish a miscreant once it is accepted that he had the freedom of will and moral autonomy to have chosen to act otherwise. However, Nietzsche argues that the idea of justice as a punitive response to moral transgression is actually 'an extremely late and refined form of human judgement and inference' that has little to do with primitive psychology (2000: 43). Punishment for primitive man – and, in fact, for much of human history – was *not* determined by the moral concept of guilt. Punishment was not a return of force – such as the imposition of a moral judgement upon an action or intention – but the primal exertion of power by a stronger over a weaker being. Later, however, punishment took on the notion of *debt*, in which a force *now* could be employed to answer or repay a prior force. From this point, punishment could develop beyond simple revenge and become the basis of a general system of right and wrong. Punishment is no longer merely the return of force upon a primary transgression; it is the force that determines a particular act *as* a crime, *as* being against the law and susceptible to sanction. Punishment becomes a *moral* force at the point where it extends beyond a specific return of force and assumes the general character of a *power to punish* transgression. Nietzsche insists that we need to resist the unhistorical idea of an original moral system of right and wrong that subsequently acquired punishment, and understand that punishment creates this system in the first place. For one only obeys or creates a law if there is some threat of punishment *and* a self who can be punished or held to be guilty. The significance of punishment is that the repayment of an earlier force gives certain acts a moral value. This is the basis of the vital connection Nietzsche adduces between (moral) guilt and (economic) debt:

> Throughout most of human history, punishment has *not* been meted out *because* the miscreant was held responsible for his act, therefore it was *not* assumed that the guilty party alone should be punished:- but rather, as parents still punish their children, it was out of anger over some wrong which had been suffered, directed at the perpetrator, – but this anger was held in check and modified by the idea that every injury has its *equivalent* which can be paid in compensation, if only through the *pain* of the person who injures. And where did this primeval, deeply-rooted and perhaps now ineradicable idea gain its power, this idea of an equivalence between injury and pain? I have already let it out: in the contractual relationship between *creditor* and *debtor*, which is as old as the very conception of a 'legal subject' and itself refers back to the basic forms of buying, selling, bartering, trade and traffic.
>
> (2000: 43)

Nietzsche establishes a connection between the 'main moral concept' of guilt and the material concept of debt in two ways. For barter and trade to be possible at all, he argues, the debtor must be able to remember his promise of remuneration; it is here that the 'hard, cruel, painful' technique of mnemonics finds its primary justification (2000: 44). In cases where a debtor is unable to repay his debt, however, a creditor is entitled to inflict all manner of mutilation and dishonour upon the debtor's body; for example, 'cutting as much flesh off as seemed appropriate for the debt', and this 'economic' bargain constituted the basis of various primitive and classical codes of law. It is this economic notion of justice that the Venetian merchant Shylock appeals to in Shakespeare's *The Merchant of Venice*, when he claims a pound of Antonio's flesh as forfeit for his failure to repay a loan. The underlying logic of such economic compensation, Nietzsche argues, was to replace repayment of goods with an increase in the creditor's feeling of power: by exercising his right to inflict pain, the creditor momentarily enjoyed the 'rights of the masters' to take pleasure in the suffering of an inferior (2000: 45). The imposition of punishment was not, then, a reaction to a violation of moral law; it was a mechanism of economic compensation by which a distinction of rank and mastery was actively enforced.

Here we arrive at one of Nietzsche's greatest challenges to the history of moral thought. The transformation of the animal 'man' into a moral being could only take place, Nietzsche claims, when the origin of our moral consciousness in cruelty and force is repressed and forgotten. This point is reached when the idea of guilt as an economic relationship between a creditor and a debtor is replaced by a *moral* interpretation that identifies guilt in the very fact of being *human*. Nietzsche's genealogy presents the historical narrative of this transformation. To appreciate the magnitude of this change, Nietzsche argues, we must recall that not only do the feelings of guilt and personal obligation originate in the economic relationship between buyer and seller; this relationship also gives each person a way of measuring themselves against others and enables the active separation of strong from weak forms of life. 'Fixing prices, setting values, working out equivalents, exchanging,' Nietzsche continues, 'this preoccupied man's first thoughts to such a degree that in a certain sense it *constitutes* thought' (2000: 49). The economic notions of calculation and exchange also lie at the origin of *justice* and *law* which are established by the most powerful natures to provide a supreme authority that prevents the weak attempting acts of revenge against the strong (2000: 53).

The economic origin of guilt, justice and law is effaced by the emergence of 'bad conscience' and the *Christian-moral* interpretation of life. With the advent of Christianity, the 'heavens darkened over man in direct proportion to the increase in his feeling shame *at being man*. . . . I mean the sickly mollycoddling and sermonizing, by means of which the animal "man" is finally taught to be ashamed of all his instincts' (2000: 46–7). The ground for this decadent transformation was supplied by the enclosure of humanity within society; now all of our instincts which could not be discharged outwardly '*turn inwards* – this is what I call the *internalization* of man: with it there now evolves in man what will later be called his "soul"' (2000: 61). The genius of Christian moralism was to reinterpret humanity's 'bad conscience' for no longer being able to live an expansive and instinctual life into a feeling of guilt and shame for being alive. The production of this profound new sense of guilt depends, Nietzsche explains, upon the reinterpretation of a finite economic relation (a debt that is, at least in theory, capable of being repaid) as the *infinite* spiritual debt of 'original sin'. Now humanity is spiritually indebted for existing at all, and the prospect of a 'once-and-for-all payment' is replaced by 'the impossibility of discharging the penance' and 'the idea that it cannot be paid off ("*eternal* punishment")' (2000: 67). It is here, Nietzsche concludes, in the emergence of a new and dominant interpretation of life, that we discover the origins of the moral concept of punishment. The 'moral' vision of 'man', like every vision of existence, represents a strategic revaluation of values that enables a particular interpretation of life to achieve pre-eminence.

ORIGIN AND PURPOSE

Nietzsche's genealogical reinterpretation of the origins of morality has had an enormous influence upon philosophical and cultural thought. One reason for this influence is Nietzsche's insistence that we need a wholly new way of understanding historical events and practices. In *On the Genealogy of Morality* he formalises many of his insights into what he terms a 'major point of historical method', which marks his genealogical rupture with traditional historiography (2000: 56). The problem with the historical accounts offered by 'moral genealogists', he insists, is that they confuse the *origin* of a practice with its *purpose*. When discussing the relationship between punishment and law, for example, they highlight a 'purpose' in punishment – such as revenge or deterrence – and then place this purpose at the beginning of law as its 'origin'. But, as Nietzsche's account of the shift between 'economic' and 'moral' interpretations of punishment demonstrates, the relationship between the origin of a practice and its ultimate purpose may lie very far apart. A properly 'genealogical' account, he suggests, would not begin by identifying the purpose and meaning of a practice at its origin before offering a narrative of its historical development. It would focus, instead, upon the systematic reinterpretation of the 'meaning' and 'purpose' of a practice according to the requirements of dominant forces:

> How have the moral geneaologists reacted so far in this matter? Naively, as is their wont: they highlight some 'purpose' in punishment, for example, revenge or deterrence, then innocently place the purpose at the start, as *causa fiendi* of punishment, and – have finished. But 'purpose in law' is the last thing we should apply to the history of the emergence of law: on the contrary, there is no more important proposition for all kinds of historical research than that which we arrive at only with great effort but which we really *should* reach, namely that the origin of the emergence of a thing and its ultimate usefulness, its practical application and incorporation into a system of ends, are *toto coelo* separate; that anything in existence, having somehow come about, is continually interpreted anew, requisitioned anew, transformed and redirected to a new purpose by a power superior to it; that everything that occurs in the organic world consists of *overpowering, dominating*, and in their turn, overpowering and dominating consist of re-interpretation, adjustment, in the process of which their former 'meaning' and 'purpose' must necessarily be obscured or completely obliterated.

(2000: 54–5)

There is no unbroken connection between the purpose or utility of a thing and the history of its emergence. The 'purpose' of a thing, Nietzsche contends, is merely the interpretation imposed upon it by a particular 'will to power'. In this sense, the 'history' of a thing or practice consists in the record of its assimilation to, and reconfiguration by, a 'greater power' – whether that be an individual, an institution or an ideology – that refashions it to meet its own needs. Consider, for example, the way the historical legacy of Shakesperean drama has been reinterpreted during the last sixty years. The significance of Lawrence Olivier's film version of *Henry V* (1944) lies predominantly in its appeal to a particular type of Englishness: the restrained, but resolute, defender of English culture whose martial vigour earned him a famous victory on foreign soil against overwhelming odds. This image of Englishness had a profound resonance for a Britain undergoing the trauma of the Second World War. The identification of 'Shakespeare' with a particular strain of the English 'character' or 'genius' was reinforced in post-war culture by Conservative politicians and newspaper editors, for whom mouthing the name 'Shakespeare' established a continuity with the glories of the Elizabethan age before the ruinous advent of cultural modernity and the creation of comprehensive schools. During the same period, however, other readers and cultural critics have drawn upon Shakespeare's the-atricality, fondness for disguise plots and fascination with statecraft and narratives of usurpation and rebellion, to ask searching questions about our perception of gender roles, sexuality and social order. The text of Shakespeare's plays remains historically constant; but their meaning and cultural resonance depends upon the contexts in which they are inter-preted and the uses to which these interpretations are put. Nietzsche anticipates this very point when he argues that the development of a 'thing' or 'tradition' should not therefore be thought of as a logical or teleological progression from an origin to the historical realisation of its meaning; it should be understood, instead, as the contingent history of its appropriation and transformation by particular forces and interests:

> So people think punishment has evolved for the purpose of punishing. But every purpose and use is just a *sign* that the will to power has achieved mastery over something less powerful, and has impressed upon it its own idea of a use func-tion; and the whole history of a 'thing', an organ, a tradition can to this extent be a continuous chain of signs, continually revealing new interpretations and adaptations, the causes of which need not be connected even amongst them-selves, but rather sometimes just follow and replace one another at random. The 'development' of a thing, a tradition, an organ is therefore certainly not its *progressus* towards a goal, still less is it a logical *progressus,* taking the shortest route with least expenditure of energy and cost – instead it is a succession of more or less profound, more or less mutually independent processes of subju-gation exacted on the thing, added to this the resistances encountered every time, the attempted transformations for the purposes of defence and reaction, and the results, too, of successful countermeasures. The form is fluid, the 'meaning' even more so . . .

(2000: 55)

SUMMARY

Nietzsche's genealogical critique examines the historical development of our moral values. It attempts to account for the emergence of these values without relying upon the prior determination of the value and nature of 'morality' and 'man'. Influenced by developments within modern philology, Nietzschean genealogy switches its analytical focus from the primordial unity of the concept or value behind a historical practice to the disparate and contingent forces that produce concepts in the first place. To this end, it marks a distinction between the origin and purpose of historical practices. A genealogical reading does not begin by identifying the purpose and meaning of a practice at its origin before offering a narrative of its historical development; it attends to the systematic reinterpretation of the 'meaning' and 'purpose' of a practice according to the requirements of dominant forces. Nietzsche's genealogical analysis of the history of morality rejects the idea of morality as an innate or natural capacity. Moral concepts are produced by successive reinterpretations of life created by dominant forces and interests.

4

HISTORY

This chapter looks more closely at Nietzsche's discovery of a 'major point of historical method' during his genealogical examination of the origins of morality. It focuses, in particular, upon the searching questions he poses to our historical sense. Throughout his writings, Nietzsche was fascinated by the question of what the *value* of history should be. We assume, Nietzsche reminds us, that to have a full and developed historical consciousness is a sign of a civilised personality. To be 'civilised' means to have at least some sense of classical and anti-quarian literature and to be aware of the great cultural heritages of antiquity. But while a developed historical consciousness may be a sign of cultural maturity, is it necessarily good for us? Is it possible that our fascination with the past has led us to be sterile and uncreative? More generally, what, Nietzsche asks, is our historical sense actually *for* and what modes of life does it make possible in the present?

THE USES OF HISTORY

These questions lie behind Nietzsche's genealogical critique of tradi-tional historiography. He undertakes this critique for three reasons. First, he seeks to undermine the humanist presumption that our values and beliefs are an expression of an essential and unhistorical human nature. Nietzsche claims, instead, that they are the creation of particular historical forces and interests. Thus he argues that 'law' and 'justice' are not the natural expression of a fundamental human need: they are interpretations of life created by a dominant force in order to set a limit to the desire for revenge felt by the inferior and weak. And as we shall see in the next chapter, Nietzsche suggests that 'morality' itself is a historically specific invention developed by the weak and resentful in order to achieve mastery over active and aristocratic being. Secondly, Nietzsche insists that the 'meaning' of history is determined by the force with which an interpretation is imposed upon life. As the history of punishment reveals, the form of a practice can remain relatively constant, but its meaning may vary greatly depending upon the uses to which it is put. It may exist to punish a moral transgression, or it may take its place within an economic system of debt and remuneration. There is no single 'purpose' that constitutes the meaning of an event; as Nietzsche will argue elsewhere, the 'meaning' of a thing 'is' the history of the interpretations that have taken hold of it. And, thirdly, Nietzsche argues that an 'interpretation' of life always expresses the force of a specific 'will to power'. For Nietzsche, forms that are taken to be constitutive of the very meaning of life – such as law, justice and morality – are interpretations imposed upon life in order that one force might assimilate the power of another to its domain. This point is implicit in the martial rhetoric of 'resistances', 'counter-measures' and 'processes of subjugation' that characterise his remarks on punishment and law quoted at the end of the last chapter (2000: 55). If 'history' is a shifting series of values and interpretations, the meaning and function of historical institutions will be determined by those who impose their will on circumstances and organise events in order to advance their own interpretation of life. His theory of 'genealogy' is therefore crucial to his belief that a 'power-will is acted out in all that happens' (2000: 56). We will explore the implications of this statement in Chapter 7.

These insights form the basis of one of Nietzsche's most influential genealogical critiques: his analysis of the historical sense in the second of his *Untimely Meditations* entitled 'On the Uses and Disadvantages of History for Life', first published in German in 1874. Nietzsche's employment in his title of a rhetoric of tactical utility – history, it is implied, has specific 'uses' which it is to the 'disadvantage' of our 'life' to neglect – immediately suggests that his critique differs markedly from other versions of historicism. The term 'historicism' describes the relationship between a particular event or structure and the historical context in which it functions. In its expressive and teleological forms, historicism is frequently employed to establish a sense of historical continuity between the past and present. An expressive version of historicism such as Ian Watt's *The Rise of the Novel* argues simultaneously that the new literary form of the novel expresses or reflects a transformation in the social structures of the world from which it emerged – the sustained focus of the novel upon individual consciousness expresses the psychological contents of the new type of 'individual' produced by mercantile capitalism – and that we continue to read novels because the culture of individualism still conditions our experience. Precisely the same form of connection is established by teleological versions of historicism, in which the interior meaning of historical consciousness is realised in the movement from a historical origin to a 'post-historical' state beyond contingency and change. Christian providential narratives, for example, discern a teleological meaning of history in the movement between humanity's fall from Paradise into contingency, change and death and the reconciliation of the sacred and mundane worlds in the apocalypse and Last Judgement. The passage of mundane time reveals glimpses of the divine pattern that will redeem it; while the 'meaning' of history is represented always and everywhere by the transition from historical consciousness to a state where history has no meaning.

Nietzsche's reflection upon the value of history marks a radical break with both these versions of historicism. He argues that the meaning of historical events is *not* determined by the broader historical context that encompasses them; nor is it the purpose of historiography simply to provide points of narrative continuity between the past and present. The point of studying history, he argues, is not to discover the 'truth' of past events; we need history 'for the sake of life and action' (1997c: 59). The fact that a particular statement concerning the past may be historically true, Nietzsche continues, is less important than that it teaches us how to live a creative and productive life *now*. He therefore extends the critique of truth and value outlined in Chapter 2 to the question of historical consciousness. The perception that something may be 'true', he argues, does not necessarily make it valuable; indeed, there are many truths that are a matter of indifference to the way we choose to live (p. 89). In fact, it is positively harmful for us to study history in the hope of acquiring as much 'general knowledge' as possible because there are many forms of knowledge – the Christian doctrine of humility and worldly renunciation, for example – that retard the development of our own capacities. For this reason, we should not turn to history in order to discover an ideal, disinterested or teleological idea of truth; we should, instead, develop a genealogical critique of *types* of historical truth that enables us to *select* those elements of the past that enable us to live productively in the present. This insight distinguishes the genealogist from the historian: the genealogist, Nietzsche claims, has the *strength* to choose between different types of historical truth in order to affirm his own perspective and values. 'We want to serve history', Nietzsche proclaims, but 'only to the extent that history serves life' (p. 59).

ACTIVE FORGETTING

Nietzsche makes this distinction between truth and value because he believes it is possible for mankind to be overburdened with history to the point where we lose our ability to enjoy independent and creative life. Nineteenth-century culture suffers from a consuming fever of history; now life has become 'stunted and degenerate' (1997c: 59). What should be borne in mind is that the nineteenth century witnessed an intense reawakening of interest in the classical cultural heritage. This fascination with classical culture lay behind the emergence of philology as an important university discipline. It was also expressed in the more general movement of *philhellenism* that emerged in Europe in the late eighteenth century, propounded by writers such as Johann Gottfried von Herder (1744–1805) and Johann Joachim Winckelmann (1717–68) and English Romantic poets such as William Blake (1757–1827), Lord Byron (1788–1824) and Percy Bysshe Shelley (1792–1822). This movement saw the perfection and nobility of Greek art as a source of eternal spiritual value that might regenerate contemporary cultural traditions. Nietzsche, we recall, was trained as a philologist, and the discipline had a profound influence upon his thought. Yet he broke with conventional philology because he could not accept this view of Hellenic culture as the repository of timeless and universal values. For Nietzsche, Greek life was driven forward by the contest between rival social and political forces. It is false, for example, to see the perfection of Greek art as the 'moral' and 'spiritual' resolution of struggle and conflict into stable cultural forms; the strength of Greek culture lay in its capacity to draw upon both the creative and destructive powers that characterise the total economy of life. Because the 'highest' values are the product of struggle and conflict, Nietzsche argues that the point of historical interest in the classical heritage is not passively to repeat or adhere to Greek values. We must learn, instead, to be as imaginative as the Greeks in *creating* our own past. For it is by struggling against and overcoming received ideas of what characterises human life and culture that we learn to develop new values.

Those who merely conform to a received idea of cultural values are unable to create a vision of life for themselves. The novelist George Eliot (1819–80) presents a vision of such an attitude in her portrait of the philologist Mr Casaubon in *Middlemarch* (1872). Casaubon's life-work is to construct the 'Key to all Mythologies': a vast historical grid intended to reveal 'that all the mythical systems or erratic mythical fragments in the world were corruptions of a tradition originally revealed' (Eliot 1994: 24). In Casaubon's view, contemporary culture is degenerate precisely to the extent it has cut itself off from the 'original' classical tradition. But as *Middlemarch* demonstrates, Casaubon's backward and nostalgic longing for the past renders him unable to live effectively within the shifting 'web' of relationships that constitute modern society. He cuts himself off from the flux of life: his intellectual inspiration deserts him, his marriage fails, and he dies unreconciled to the world around him.

Casaubon's fate illustrates the peril of submerging our individuality within too full a sense of the historical past. Nietzsche contrasts the sterility and unhappiness of human life weighed down by historical consciousness with the image of cattle grazing happily in a field. Why, he asks, despite our evident superiority as a species, do we envisage the happiness of these animals as a 'lost paradise' (1997c: 61)? Because their incomprehension of the burden of the past allows them to live *unhistorically* and contentedly in the present. Nietzsche accepts that this absolutely unhistorical sense is an inadequate model for humanity because we are defined as a social species by our capacity for dissimulation and a degree of self-consciousness – including our consciousness of death – which teaches us that existence is 'a thing that lives by negating, consuming and contradicting itself' (p. 61). Yet to abandon ourselves passively to the relentless pressure of the past means to submerge our identity beneath the multitude of interpretations of the world that have already been established. We would then experience history like the idle and motiveless tourist who 'hungry for distraction or excitement, prowls around as though among pictures in a gallery' (p. 68).

The solution Nietzsche proposes to this dilemma is for humanity *actively to forget* the burden of the historical past in the act of creating its own vision of the world. Active forgetting and the cultivation of the unhistorical sense are 'essential to action of any kind' (1997c: 62). In fact, Nietzsche argues, the capacity to feel unhistorically is constitutive of our historical sense as such. If we did not choose to embrace certain aspects of past experience at the expense of others, we would drown in a pure 'stream of becoming' and our historical consciousness would lose all shape and coherence. Too full a historical sense destroys the concept of 'history' itself. Nietzsche formalises this insight in the more general observation that 'there is a degree of sleeplessness, of rumination, of the historical sense, which is harmful and ultimately fatal to the living thing, whether this living thing be a man or a people or a culture' (p. 62).

Both the 'unhistorical' and the 'historical' senses are necessary, Nietzsche argues, to the health of an individual, a people and a culture. The genealogist is an untimely thinker not just because he challenges conventional readings of the past, but because he acknowledges the importance of the unhistorical sense to the creation of historical values. For modern culture to draw productively upon the past, various types of historical experience must be repressed and forgotten. Nietzsche's genealogical readings focus repeatedly upon the status of 'history' as a process of *selection* and *repression* because it underlines the connection between forms of life and modes of power. A certain form of life – like Christianity or modern political democracy – becomes powerful by possessing the strength to act unhistorically and overcome the burden of history, effect a radical break with the past, and assert its own values. The truly strong nature appropriates what it needs from history in order to create the most productive conditions for its own existence. To do so, it must set a limit to the flux of history by enclosing life within a bounded 'horizon' (1997c: 63). Once this horizon has been established, it becomes possible to create a balance between those features of histor-ical consciousness that help to produce us as human – such as the ability to think and reflect self-consciously upon experience – and the restraining boundary of the unhistorical sense:

Cheerfulness, the good conscience, the joyful deed, confidence in the future – all of them depend, in the case of the individual as of a nation, on the existence of a line dividing the bright and discernible from the unilluminable and dark; on one's being just as able to forget at the right time as to remember at the right time; on the possession of a powerful instinct for sensing when it is necessary to feel historically and when unhistorically. This precisely, is the proposition the reader is invited to meditate upon: *the unhistorical and the historical are necessary in equal measure for the health of an individual, of a people and of a culture.*

(1997c: 63)

HISTORICAL TYPES

In contrast to traditional historiography, Nietzsche's genealogical reading of the past concentrates upon the different ways history becomes *useful* to humanity. This emphasis upon the utility, rather than the 'objective' value, of history culminates in his presentation of a genealogical critique of historical types. Nietzsche identifies three principle forms in which mankind makes use of the past: monumental, antiquarian and critical history. The 'monumental' conception of history is developed typically by the 'man of action' appalled by the decadence and narcissism of contemporary culture (1997c: 68). It seeks to arrest this decline by reviving whatever in the past expanded and ennobled the concept of 'man'. The fundamental aim of the monumental historian is to reproduce the great moments of the past within the present; this aim may be realised, he believes, because 'the great moments in the struggle of the human individual constitute a chain' that 'unites mankind across the millennia like a range of human mountain peaks' (p. 68). The values of antiquarian history, meanwhile, are expressed in a profound reverence for the past and the desire to determine the significance of the present from its position within a continuous national tradition. The antiquarian sense is developed typically by scholars and political conservatives, and it is this view of the past 'which is today usually designated as the real sense of history' (p. 74). Finally, Nietzsche turns to critical history, which he defines as a history that 'judges and condemns' (p. 72). The critical historian arraigns the past before the tribunal of the *present* in order to establish which of its aspects might assist us in creating strong and productive conditions for life. To do so, he must 'possess and from time to time employ the strength to break up and dissolve a part of the past' (p. 75). A critical history is not therefore governed by abstract ideals of truth, justice and fidelity to tradition.

It discerns value only in those historical forces that serve 'life alone, that dark, driving power that insatiably thirsts for itself' (p. 76).

It is clear from this synopsis that the question posed by genealogical critique – how do we produce the version of the past that serves life by expanding our productive capacities? – finds its most fruitful response in a critical history. This impression is reinforced by the deficiencies Nietzsche detects in the monumental and antiquarian alternatives. The weakness of a monumental history is twofold: it glibly assumes that the values of one age are possible and productive in another; and this emphasis upon the timeless persistence of epochal moments retards the active creation of new values and forms of life. These deficiencies are compounded by the 'backward glance' of antiquarian history which routinely privileges every event that is subservient to a tradition at the expense of both 'higher life' and newly emerging historical forces (1997c: 75). An antiquarian history 'knows only how to *preserve* life, not how to engender it'. Nietzsche's point, however, is that despite these shortcomings we must preserve the monumental and antiquarian sense and supplement them with the rigour of critical history. A genealogist can only produce an image of the past to suit mankind's present and future needs if he understands the historical constitution of its traditions and values. Once monumental and antiquarian knowledge is refined from the perspective of the present by the critical sense of judgement, we can create a new *version* of the past to inaugurate new visions of life:

> For since we are the outcome of earlier generations, we are also the outcome of their aberrations, passions and errors, and indeed of their crimes; it is not possible wholly to free oneself from this chain. If we condemn these aberrations and regard ourselves as free of them, this does not alter the fact that we originate in them. The best we can do is to confront our inherited and hereditary nature with our knowledge, and through a new, stern discipline, combat our inborn heritage and implant in ourselves a new habit, a new instinct, a second nature, so that our first nature withers away. It is an attempt to give oneself, as it were *a posteriori*, a past in which one would like to originate in opposition to that in which one did originate . . .
>
> (1997c: 76)

MODERNITY AND STYLE

Nietzsche's conviction that the proper function of historical knowledge is 'always and only for the ends of life' underlies his critique of *modernity* (1997c: 77). One reason for the weakness of modern culture, he argues, is that the role of historical knowledge in producing strong forms of life has been transformed by the demand that history should be a *science*. Once this transformation occurs, knowledge is robbed of both its historical specificity and its role in creating values; now knowledge is only deemed valuable if it conforms to the criterion of universal and objective truth. But knowledge can only be useful to mankind, Nietzsche insists, if it is put to work within the 'horizon' of a particular form of historical life (p. 63). The schism between a vision of history

MODERNITY

Despite a vast number of conflicting definitions, modernity is usually identified with the shift from external to internal authority. Philosophers such as Thomas Hobbes (1588–1679) and René Descartes (1596–1650) no longer relied on God or concepts of divine order to establish what was true. Instead, philosophers and scientists insisted that authority needed to be established from what was verifiable, human and subject to human reason. The Enlightenment movements of the eighteenth century insisted that if a claim were true, then it could be demonstrated and justified; no one ought simply to accept received wisdom, tradition or already established hierarchies. Whereas *modernity* is defined from the sixteenth century onwards, *modernism* is usually used to define the artistic movements of the twentieth century that expressed a disillusionment in the supreme values of reason and humanity to which modernity appealed. The supposed universal subject of reason who could replace external authority was recognised as one more myth of authority. Modernist writers such as James Joyce (1882–1941), Virginia Woolf (1882–1941) and T. S. Eliot (1888–1965) described a human subject not of judgement and reason, but of fluid impressions, disruptive desires, primitive forces, unconscious motivations, bodily affects and streams of sense impressions. Modernism was therefore an extension of modernity insofar as it was critical of received and fixed forms. But it was also critical of modernity insofar as it abandoned any belief in substituting an internal and human authority for traditional external authorities.

governed by the 'demands of life' and its new incarnation in a 'science of universal becoming' creates the defining feature of modern experience: the ceaseless production of objective and valueless 'knowledge' which 'no longer acts as an agent for transforming the outside world but remains concealed within a chaotic inner world which modern man describes with a curious pride as his uniquely characteristic inwardness' (pp. 77–8).

Nietzsche's critique of modernity was shared by some of the major modernist writers. In his poem *The Waste Land* (1922), T. S. Eliot focused upon exactly the schism Nietzsche identified between objective and valueless 'knowledge' and the chaotic inner world of modern humanity. Eliot's apocalyptic vision of modern Europe is of a landscape in which traditional values and social structures are in turmoil. The throbbing unrest and directionlessness of modern culture are a consequence, Eliot suggests, of our alienation from both the Judeao-Christian heritage and the values of classical European culture. All around him Eliot sees evidence of 'cracks' and 'falling towers', and this disintegration is thematised explicitly in cultural and spiritual terms: 'Cracks and reforms and bursts in the violet air | Falling towers | Jerusalem Athens Alexandria | Vienna London | Unreal' (Eliot 1977: 73). In place of a secure sense of cultural and spiritual value symbolised by the great cities of western learning, all we have now is the formlessness and chaos of random and unstructured historical forces. *The Waste Land* reproduces this historical chaos stylistically by its relentless juxtaposition of different languages, traditions and registers outside any shared cultural narrative that might order them into sense: the Greek seer Tiresias rubs shoulders with the fake modern clairvoyant Madame Sosostris, while Shakespearean English blurs into the cacophony of a contemporary London pub. Gazing out over London Bridge, the poet sees only commuters enduring a living death: 'A crowd flowed over London Bridge, so many, | I had not thought death had undone so many' (1977: 62). The modern citizen is 'dead', Eliot believes, because she has subordinated the spiritual and moral dimension of life to the merely mundane knowledge of bourgeois 'progress' and social advancement. The elevation of temporal and secular beliefs over spiritual needs ensures a division between the lifeless external face we turn to the world and our repressed inner self that longs for spiritual redemption and release. This separation of the inner world of feeling from the outer world of action is captured perfectly in the loveless exchange between the bored typist and her 'young man carbuncular', whose 'vanity requires no response | and makes a welcome of indifference' (p. 68).

For Nietzsche, like Eliot, the definitive modern disjunction between the chaotic inner world of our feelings and desires and the bland outward form we present to the world is the consequence of our prostration before an endless 'stream of new things' and our inability to determine the utility of different forms of historical knowledge (1997c: 79). Where Nietzsche differs profoundly from Eliot, of course, is in the solution he proposes to our unhappy modern state. We should not, in Nietzsche's view, look for answers to the problems of modern life in a resurgent Christian moralism; the subordination of life to a moral law based upon humility and the interests of the weak was, for Nietzsche, precisely what robbed classical culture of its vital force. What modernity lacks is not the imposition of a transcendent moral law, but rather that sense of *aesthetic style*, typified for Nietzsche by the Greeks, which combines the interests of public and private life by incorporating into contemporary consciousness only those historical forces that meet the needs of a people.

ASCENT AND DESCENT

For this new style of being to develop, the genealogist must develop a version of history that appropriates the past in order to transform contemporary life. To 'appropriate' that past does not mean merely to judge it by the trivial standards of current morality; it means to reinterpret the past to meet the needs of the *strongest* and most *creative* spirits of the present. 'If you are to venture to interpret the past,' Nietzsche declares, 'you can do so only out of the fullest exertion of the vigour of the present' (1997c: 94). The point of historical 'interpretation' in the genealogical sense is to determine whether our values reflect an *ascending* or *descending* form of life: either a way of living in which active forces are harmoniously integrated or a weak and degenerate mode of existence dominated by the values and prejudices of the past. Because the responsibility for choosing between different historical truths always involves a distinction between ascending and descending modes of life, Nietzsche claims that it 'can be borne only by strong personalities, weak ones are utterly extinguished by it' (p. 86). The strong personality accepts that 'objectivity' and 'justice' are incompatible values in historical terms because the value of historical analysis from a genealogical perspective has little to do with the enumeration of empirical facts or the fulfilment of general propositions. Its *real* value is to confer a purposive shape upon the past so that we might distinguish between ascending and descending life and 'to inspire and lend the strength for the production of the great man' (p. 111).

What Nietzsche calls 'positive' historical objectivity is this affirmation of the ascending and active force of life (1997c: 93). His idea of a 'higher man' is not, it should be noted, a racial concept, despite its subsequent appropriation by Nazi ideologues. To cultivate a 'higher' being, as we will see in Chapter 5, is to select and give coherence to an ascending movement of life. Without some notion of higher and active being, Nietzsche argues, all we see around us is 'immoderate revelling in the process [of becoming] at the expense of being and life, the senseless displacement of all perspectives' (p. 112). Such bland endorsement of the general fact of historical change culminates, he concludes, in an empty relativism that no longer possesses the power to create new values and distinctions. In contrast, Nietzsche's assertion that the proper function of history is to enable mankind to *overcome* morality and produce an image of a 'higher' life beyond good and evil is fundamental to his idea of a *great politics*. His emphasis upon both the pragmatic and creative nature of historical 'truth' extends his analysis of metaphor insofar as history ultimately becomes a self-conscious and productive fiction designed to 'remint the universally known into something never heard of before' and establish the genealogist as an 'architect of the future' (p. 94). Moreover, his self-consciously aesthetic vision of history as a purposive and coherent reworking of the past reveals the particular *historical* origins of every historical narrative – the recognition that the past is *always* reinterpreted according to present interests and demands – and lays bare its role in the development of specific values and forms of life. Once we accept the historical constitution of historical 'truth', it becomes possible to see our values as an effect of the will to power of dominant social groupings such as the church, aristocracy or the ruling class. These values no longer appear 'natural' or 'timeless', but rather the consequence of violence, conflict and a struggle for authority between competing interpretations of life. The task for us *now*, Nietzsche insists, is to move *beyond* the exhausted and declining Judaeo-Christian vision of existence and create a new interpretation of life for the future. He undertook this labour in his critique of morality and the ascetic life, to which we turn in Chapter 5.

SUMMARY

Nietzsche's genealogical reading of history argues that the meaning of history is determined by the force with which an interpretation of the past is imposed upon life. There is no single idea or purpose that constitutes the meaning of an historical event; the meaning of an idea or practice is produced by the history of interpretations that have taken hold of it. Because history is a shifting series of values and interpretations, the meaning and function of historical institutions will be determined by those who impose their will on circumstances and organise events in order to advance their own interpretation of life. The point of studying history for Nietzsche is not to discover the immutable historical 'truth' of past events; we need to develop an interpretation of the past that enables us to live powerfully and productively in the present.

5

BEYOND GOOD
AND EVIL

In this chapter we will look more closely at Nietzsche's development of an 'immoral' philosophy beyond good and evil. Nietzsche's *On the Genealogy of Morality* provided a genealogy of the development of 'man' as a moral being. It did so to demonstrate the historical character of our values and moral beliefs and, beyond this, to argue that 'morality' is itself a belated reinterpretation of a system of arbitrary acts of cruelty and force. A punitive regime of retribution is developed to create mankind's memory and its historical consciousness of debt; the external and violent origins of memory are then gradually effaced and become internalised as 'conscience', and the image of 'man' as a creature with a *natural* moral capacity is born. Morality is, in this sense, merely the story we tell ourselves about our lowly and immoral origins.

The history of mankind is therefore inseparable from a process of *moralisation* designed to efface the origins of our values in violence and cruelty and produce an image of moral 'man'. Nietzsche's critique of this moralising process develops by placing in question the value of foundational moral concepts like 'good' and 'evil'. This is one of the most notorious issues in Nietzsche's work, because it is linked to his idea of an 'immoral' style of living. From his childhood Nietzsche was fascinated by 'the question of *what origin* our terms good and evil actually have' (2000: 5). Soon his preoccupation with this problem was transformed into a more general question: 'Under what conditions did man invent the value judgements good and evil? *and what value do they themselves have?'* (p. 5). Does what we call 'goodness' promote the interests of mankind by enabling us to express our courage, creativity, vitality and embrace an *ascending* and expansive mode of life? Or might 'goodness' be a mode of *descent* and a sign of the degeneration of life by confining our experience within narrow and outmoded moral parameters and retarding our ability to create our own values? What if a regressive trait lurked within the 'good man' so that 'morality itself was the danger of dangers?' (p. 8). Is it possible to imagine a life *beyond* the moral opposition of 'good' and 'evil'? What would such a life look like?

These are troubling questions intended to shake the foundations of our entire religious and moral heritage. Nietzsche's examination of the *value* of morality begins with an analysis of pity and altruism. We habitually assume that to pity the unfortunate and consider the interests of others are good and virtuous acts. An assumption shared by both Christian ethics and philosophers such as Jean-Jacques Rousseau (1712–78) is that moral virtues are synonymous with love of one's neighbour and a charitable attitude towards the weak. To put the interests of another before one's own indicates a quality of natural goodness and may well earn the selfless heavenly reward. However, Nietzsche's critique of moral values challenges the priority granted to the instincts of pity and self-sacrifice in the conduct of human affairs (2000: 7). He argues that far from exhibiting moral strength, the 'cult of pity' is a sign of mankind's exhaustion and its renunciation of will. Moral virtue only becomes associated with pity and selflessness, he continues, when mankind no longer feels able to overcome its own history and create new values. This moral revaluation is an effect of the triumph of the weak over the strong demonstrated by what Nietzsche calls the 'slave revolt in morals'. In this revolt the weak cultivate pity and humility to elevate their own incapacity for effective action into a form of virtue. The establishment of altruism as an absolute moral virtue also forms the basis for political movements like social democracy, which Nietzsche depicts as a conspiracy of the weak against those strong and noble natures capable of asserting their will to power and imposing their own values on the world.

Nietzsche's reflection on the elevation of moral altruism develops two insights crucial to his ideal of an immoral philosophy beyond good and evil. First, he argues that the morality of pity is *not* selfless but rather embodies a weak and reactive will to power intended to subordinate the strong to the weak and preserve a degenerating form of life. For the feeling of pity always involves a degree of contempt for the person pitied; and this pleasurable experience of superiority enables the 'altruistic' individual to believe itself more powerful than before. Postcolonial critics, for example, have argued that the western circulation of pitiable images of Third-World suffering – such as pictures of starving African children – does not fulfil a humanitarian impulse; the point of these images of helpless victimhood is to demonstrate that 'we' can help those unable to help themselves and constitute ourselves as ethical and powerful in the process. In *Beyond Good and Evil*, Nietzsche contends that the weak nature *requires* this reactive reference to a pitiable figure in order to constitute its own identity; this assertion lies at the heart of his theory of *ressentiment*. The noble nature, by contrast, is '*not* made for pity' because it has the strength spontaneously to affirm its own nature (1990a: 196). Secondly, the recognition that slave morality *develops* a cult of pity illuminates for Nietzsche the historical character of our moral values. We are mistaken to believe that attitudes such as pity and egoism are *naturally* good or evil; these moral interpretations are retrospectively affixed by dominant social groupings to justify their own mode of existence. Before values come into existence there is the struggle for mastery between strong and weak forces. Nietzsche's 'immoral' philosophy seeks to overcome the reactive morality of 'good' and 'evil' imposed by the weak and to inaugurate a new era of aristocratic values.

MASTER MORALITY AND SLAVE MORALITY

Nietzsche develops his critique of the moral priority of selfless and unegoistic actions by examining the relationship between custom and morality. He focuses initially upon what he calls the 'pre-moral period of mankind' when values were determined by the force of local custom and tradition rather than the modern dichotomy of good and evil (1990a: 63). To be 'ethical' or 'correct' in these societies, he notes in *Human, All Too Human*, meant to obey an 'age-old law or tradition' rather than an abstract moral ideal (1984: 66). Because traditional communities made no reference to individual moral autonomy or intention, it did not matter whether or not one endorsed a particular law; it was enough that one *submitted* to it. Where these communities distinguished between good and harmful actions 'the basic opposition is not "egoism" and "self-lessness", but rather adherence to a tradition or law, and release from it' (pp. 66–7). A particular action was deemed right or wrong according to the dictate of customs which took *habit* as their condition of existence: 'since lower peoples and cultures have only very slight insight into the real causality, they make sure, with a superstitious fear, that everything takes the same course; even where a custom is difficult, harsh, burdensome, it is preserved because it seems to be highly useful' (pp. 67–8). To be released from communal bonds and obligations and become an individual in this world was not a sign of progress but a form of punishment; indeed, the 'individual' – the figure whose tastes and qualities modern culture is always seeking to develop – was a species of *outlaw* who lacked the strength to endure the 'proven wisdom' of the tribe (p. 67).

However, the weakness of traditional communities based upon the laws of custom lies precisely in the fact that they 'force each individual' in the community to accept 'the same mores' (1984: 67). Such compulsion is anathema to strong or 'aristocratic' natures which exist to create their own laws as an effect of their superabundant power and creativity. An aristocratic society, Nietzsche claims in *Beyond Good and Evil*, demands instead that 'pathos of distance' that separates strong from weak natures and enables the powerful to 'overcome' the morality of all previous forms of life:

> Every elevation of the type 'man' has hitherto been the work of an aristocratic society – and so it will always be: a society which believes in a long scale of orders or rank and differences of worth between man and man and needs slavery in some sense or other. Without the *pathos of distance* such as develops from the incarnate differences of classes, from the ruling caste's constant looking out and looking down on subjects and instruments and from its equally constant exercise of obedience and command, its holding down and holding at a distance, that other, more mysterious pathos could not have developed either, that longing for an ever-increasing widening of distance within the soul itself, the formation of ever-higher, rarer, more remote, tenser, more comprehensive states, in short precisely the elevation of the type 'man', the continual 'self-overcoming of man', to take a moral formula in a supra-moral sense.
>
> (1990a: 192)

Here we approach the heart of Nietzsche's philosophy. The supreme value of an aristocratic society is its demand that humanity overcomes itself by cultivating its power and authority over 'weaker' forms of life. Whereas moral and altruistic perspectives – such as Christianity, socialism and certain forms of modern political democracy – seek to reduce this difference in rank, aristocratic culture exacerbates it. Indeed, what Nietzsche calls 'power' is measured by the distance created between strong and weak natures. Nietzsche relishes the shock provoked by his statement that the truly aristocratic society 'requires slavery in some sense'. However, he insists that social structures based on a moral appeal to 'equal rights' or the 'common good' *also* require violence to achieve their aims: the calculated repression of the aristocratic nature who refuses to accept shared judgements and moral values.

The creation of an aristocratic order of rank represents the first stage in the overcoming of the pre-moral life of the community of custom. Nietzsche is unflinching in his account of the violent usurpation of authority by aristocratic 'men of prey' replete with 'an unbroken strength of will and lust for power' as they 'threw themselves upon weaker, more civilised, more peaceful, perhaps trading or cattle-raising races, or upon old mellow cultures, the last vital forces in which were even then flickering out in a glittering firework display of spirit and corruption' (1990a: 192). This noble type of man 'feels *himself* to be the determiner of values' because he does not need to be approved by tradition or any other form of law: he *creates* the values by which he lives (p. 195). His wilful independence from external constraint is reinforced by his creation of a set of 'moral value-distinctions' that express his superiority to weak and slavish natures. These distinctions are underpinned by a moral division between 'good' and 'bad' types of being:

> The man who has the power to requite goodness with goodness, evil with evil, and really does practice requital by being grateful and vengeful, is called 'good'. The man who is unpowerful and cannot requite is taken for bad. As a good man, one belongs to the 'good', a community that has a communal feeling, because all the individuals are entwined together by their feeling for requital. As a bad man, one belongs to the 'bad', to a mass of abject, powerless men who have no communal feeling. The good men are a caste; the bad men are a multitude, like particles of dust. Good and bad are for a time equivalent to noble and base, master and slave.
>
> (1984: 47)

What Nietzsche means by the 'good' man, as we noted in Chapter 3, is a powerful figure of aristocratic self-possession who has an *active* sense of value because he determines them according to the needs of his own nature. To be 'good' is to possess the capacity to rule and command (including self-command and self-discipline); this is the distinguishing feature of every noble and masterful nature. These noble natures are blessed with an overabundance of will and vitality which they exploit to construct a world in their own image. Their sense of themselves as 'good' and 'noble' arises spontaneously from their impression of their own power and creativity; the designation of other beings as 'bad', 'low' or 'slavish' only occurs subsequently as a way of distinguishing them from the aristocratic order. Nietzsche's term *master morality* describes the independent and spontaneous self-affirmation of noble nature in its distinction from every other form of life. It therefore differs markedly from 'common-sense' conceptions of morality as impersonal and universal views about human actions and motivations. The creation of moral values as an expression of a particular *type* of being is, he argues, the forgotten *origin* of morality. Familiarity with aristocratic societies like ancient Greece reveals that 'designations of moral value were everywhere first applied to *human beings*, and only later and derivatively to *actions*' (1990a: 195). It is only in more recent times that action and attitudes such as 'pity', 'selflessness' and hostility to suffering have been detached from the fundamental question of the nobility or baseness of one's being and become the determining ground of moral values. Today violence, cruelty and the infliction of suffering are condemned as uncharitable and unchristian; but for aristocratic cultures they were part of a broader economy of life which took as its goal the production of a *higher* type of 'man':

> To refrain from mutual injury, mutual violence, mutual exploitation, to equate one's own will with that of another: this may in a certain rough sense become good manners between individuals if the conditions for it are present (namely if their strength and value standards are in fact similar and they both belong to one body). As soon as there is a desire to take this principle further, however, and if possible even as the *fundamental principle of society*, it at once reveals itself as the will to the *denial* of life, as the principle of dissolution and decay. One has to think this matter thoroughly through to the bottom and resist all sentimental weakness: life itself is *essentially* appropriation, injury, overpowering of the strange and weaker, incorporation and, at the least and mildest, exploitation . . .

(1990a: 193–4)

The drive implicit within master morality to overcome inferior forms of life should not be interpreted as an apology for random violence; it underpins a *moral* and *aesthetic* vision of a noble style of living. The duty of every noble nature, Nietzsche makes clear in *Human, All Too Human* is to 'make a noble *person* of oneself' (1984: 66). This aim may only be achieved by the noble human being who 'has power over himself, who understands how to speak and how to keep silent, who enjoys practising severity and harshness upon himself and feels reverence for all that is severe and harsh' (1990a: 196). The noble 'pathos of distance' calls for 'an ever-increasing widening of distance within the soul itself' and thus demands that continual self-overcoming and perfection of one's own nature which only the masterful being can sustain (p. 192).

The 'good' or noble man, then, simply affirms his own super-fluity of power; all distinctions of caste and rank are determined by the degree to which others are able to reproduce this act of self-legitimation. The 'bad' man, by contrast, is a base and slavish figure unable to determine the conditions of his own existence. All of his values are *reactive;* they are defined by their *opposition* to aristocratic values rather than by their potential to create their own world. Consequently, the 'bad' live in a state of festering resentment towards the 'good'. The 'bad' man can create nothing from his own nature; his is a secondary and derivative form of life defined by the lack of noble qualities such as strength, creativity and self-affirmation. Slavish nature is envious and mistrustful of everything 'good' and strives to reinter-pret the instinctive and unconscious self-possession of aristocratic nature as stupidity and lack of guile; meanwhile it cultivates every quality (like pity, humility, patience and industriousness) that might alleviate the burden of its existence.

A decisive shift in moral history occurs at the point when slavish nature develops a vision of 'man' to challenge the power and pre-eminence of aristocratic being: this is the emergence of *slave morality*. But although the appearance of slave morality is a revolutionary event, Nietzsche argues that it is also a pernicious and destructive phenomenon that has had catastrophic consequences for the human condition. The reason for this is that slave morality emerges as a state of impotent and resentful opposition to aristocratic values rather than as a creative expression of a new vision of life. The parasitic dependence of slave morality upon aristocratic values is implicit in its revaluation of the moral dichotomy 'good' and 'bad' as 'good and 'evil'. Slavish nature is incapable of overcoming morality from a position of strength; instead, it first defines its enemy as 'evil' in order that it might then equate its own weakness with the 'good'.

Modern historians and psychologists, Nietzsche suggests, profoundly misapprehend the evolution of moral ideas. Their account claims that originally unegoistic and selfless actions were valued by the people to whom they were useful; later this origin of moral ideas was forgotten as people began to value certain actions according to their customary reputation and eventually they were simply declared good *as such* (2000: 12). But this view of history is only possible as a consequence of the decline of aristocratic values. For the judgement 'good' was *not* originally bestowed by those to whom goodness was shown; it arose from the noble pathos of distance that distinguished between superior and inferior modes of being. It required the slave revolt in morality for qualities like pity, humility and patience to be transformed into the 'good' while expressions of aristocratic being like power, expansiveness and physical vitality were condemned as harmful to the body politic. In its opposition to the elite order of aristocratic being, slave morality manifests itself as a form of *herd instinct* by which the weak bond together to contest the authority of the noble spirit (p. 13). This challenge depends in turn upon a moral division between 'egoistic' and 'unegoistic' drives – the former now being conceived as 'evil' and the latter as 'good' – that has no meaning within aristocratic culture where being is the natural and spontaneous expression of the will to accumulate and expend force and energy.

RESSENTIMENT

Nietzsche argues that the radical break with aristocratic values represented by the slave revolt in morality is defined by the principle of *ressentiment*. The life of the weak individual is dominated by a sense of impotence and the inability to express itself in effective action. To compensate for this inadequacy, slavish nature devises an 'imaginary revenge' on noble and higher life (2000: 21). Where aristocratic values were bred from the experience of the natural plenitude and self-sufficiency of the noble spirit, slavish life can only create a moral vision by saying 'No' to everything outside itself. Because slavish being is unable simply to affirm its *own* life and values, it is compelled to redirect the 'evaluating glance' of moral judgement *outward* on to a world it finds hostile and superior to itself (p. 21). *Ressentiment* describes the movement in which this reactive and resentful denial of higher life begins to *create* its own moral system and vision of the world. Slave morality is a form of moral recoil from life; it can only create a vision of existence by first projecting an 'opposing, external world' that represses the weak and vulnerable. Like every manifestation of *ressentiment*, slave morality 'needs, physiologically speaking, external stimuli in order to act at all – its action is basically a reaction' (p. 22). The noble spirit develops its aristocratic pathos of distance by first asserting its own power and then marking each degree of its difference from the surrounding world. The slavish type needs, however, to create the image of the 'evil' man of power in order to define itself as a 'good' moral subject. This need perhaps explains our endless fascination with the artistic depiction of villains and forces of evil: the ruthless invaders of science fiction films and the Iagos of tragedy. We recoil from their malignity and through this movement of renunciation create an ethical image of 'us' opposed to a pervasive and inhuman evil.

Nietzsche detects the spirit of *ressentiment* in every attempt by a weak force to make life conform to a general and abstract system of values. He suggests in *The Antichrist* that injustice 'never lies in unequal rights; it lies in the claim to "*equal*" rights' (1990b: 191). Nietzsche rejects any moral or political appeal to equality (implicit within bodies of thought like socialism, feminism and the democratic ethos) because the rights due to each individual cannot be defined by a universal law but are 'determined by the nature of his being' (p. 191). Similarly, he condemns beliefs such as Christianity and anti-Semitism which, he claims, develop 'from weakness, from envy, from *vengefulness*'. He reserves particular scorn for Christianity because it dismisses 'all that represents the *ascending* movement of life, well-constitutedness, power, beauty, self-affirmation on earth' in order to 'invent *another* world from which that *life-affirmation* would appear evil, reprehensible as such' (pp. 146–7). Christianity is not merely one form of *ressentiment*; it represents *ressentiment* in its most developed phase by organising 'a revolt of everything that crawls along the ground directed against that which is *elevated*' (p. 169). Life is an 'instinct for growth, for continuance, for accumulation of forces'; Nietzsche continues, 'where the will to power is lacking there is decline' (p. 129). Viewed in this context, Christianity represents both the spirit of *ressentiment* and of historical decadence:

> One should not embellish or dress up Christianity: it has waged a *war to the death* against this *higher* type of man, it has excommunicated all the fundamental instincts of this type, it has distilled evil, the *Evil One*, out of these instincts – the strong human being as the type of reprehensibility, as the 'outcast'. Christianity has taken the side of everything weak, base, ill-constituted, it has made an ideal out of *opposition* to strong life; it has depraved the reason even of the intellectually strongest natures by teaching men to feel the supreme values of intellectuality as sinful, as misleading, as *temptations*.
>
> (1990b: 129)

Although there had been challenges to Christianity since the Enlightenment, with thinkers like Voltaire (1694–1778) in the eighteenth century pointing out the ways in which religion lulled the populace into an illusory happiness, Nietzsche's thought is quite different. Nietzsche's interpretation of Christianity as *ressentiment* does not just expose religion as an illusion imposed from without; it examines the will and desire of those who accede to this illusion. For the spirit of *ressentiment* happily debases itself before an external law in order to maintain itself in a weak state.

Nietzsche's analysis of *ressentiment* is also remarkable for the light it sheds upon the historical origins of *justice*. A prejudice common to certain political attitudes – Nietzsche refers specifically to 'anarchists' and 'anti-Semites' – is to sanctify revenge with the name 'justice', as though justice 'were fundamentally simply a further development of the feeling of having been wronged' (2000: 52). Nietzsche challenges this reactive account of the beginnings of justice in *ressentiment* by presenting another explanation of the origin of justice, which sees it developing from 'actual *active* emotions such as lust for power and possessions and the like' (p. 52). He extends this idea by identifying the origins of justice in a form of economic and military settlement. For the noble spirit, Nietzsche claims, justice had no connection with either revenge or altruistic and selfless notions of fairness and rights; it was a mode of *exchange* between roughly equal and opposed aristocratic powers. Where both military parties were equally matched, and no clear resolution to a dispute could be reached, the prospect of prolonged and bloody conflict was averted by the reciprocal exchange of goods. For this reason the 'initial character' of justice is barter, negotiation and exchange rather than an abstract and purely formal idea of equality (1984: 64):

> Historically speaking, justice on earth represents ... the battle, then, against *reactive* sentiment, the war waged against the same on the part of active and aggressive forces, which have partly expended their strength in trying to put a stop to the spread of reactive pathos, to keep it in check and within bounds, and to force some kind of compromise with it. Everywhere that justice is practised and maintained, the stronger powers can be seen looking for means of putting an end to the senseless ravages of *ressentiment* amongst those inferior to it (whether groups or individuals), partly by lifting the object of *ressentiment* out of the hands of revenge, partly by substituting, for revenge, a struggle against the enemies of peace and order, partly by working out compensation, suggesting, sometimes enforcing it, and partly by promoting certain equivalences for wrongs into a norm which *ressentiment*, from now on, has to take into account.
>
> (2000: 53)

The most decisive imposition of norms to prevent the entrenchment of *ressentiment* within moral and political thought is the establishment of law and a legal system (2000: 54). As we saw in Chapter 3, the law comes into force to challenge the resentful account of justice that interprets every action from the perspective of the injured party. Consequently, it is vacuous in historical terms to talk of actions being *essentially* 'just' or 'unjust'; these terms only become meaningful *after* the institution of a legal system. The fact that justice originates in a system designed by the strong to resist the *ressentiment* of the weak does not mean, however, that it represents a final and elevated stage in mankind's development. From the point of view of noble life, states of legality 'can never be anything but *exceptional states*, since they are partial restrictions of the true will of life, which is bent upon power, and are subordinate to its ultimate goal as a single means: namely, as a means of creating *bigger* units of power' (p. 54). The truly noble spirit lives beyond every established ideal of good and evil and remains indifferent to slights and personal injury. Such 'self-sublimation of justice' constitutes the 'prerogative of the most powerful man, better still, his way of being beyond the law' (p. 52).

FREE WILL AND THE MORAL SUBJECT

The life of the aristocratic spirit returns justice to its proper basis as the natural expression of noble *being*. Nietzsche presents the superabundant vitality of noble being in his infamous nomadic figure of the *'blond beast'* whom he pictures 'avidly prowling round for spoil and victory' in the grip of a freedom 'from every social constraint' (2000: 25). The blond beast abjures the slavish ethic of pity and charity; it lives beyond good and evil and every moral interpretation of humanity. Nietzsche does not employ the epithet 'blond' to denote a specifically *racial* concept – the beast's heritage is variously 'Roman, Arabian, Germanic, Japanese nobility, Homeric heroes, Scandinavian Vikings' – but to describe a radical element of force and transfiguration (p. 25). The blond beast lives a life of *affirmation* by challenging and overcoming the morality of custom in the name of expansiveness and acquisition. For this reason, Nietzsche argues, it is in the interest of slavish nature and every reactive culture to transform this wild nature into a 'tame and civilised animal' and an 'instrument of culture' so that weakness may be established as the universal condition of 'man' (p. 26). This transformation is accomplished by two of the most brilliant innovations of slave morality: the invention of 'free will' and the fiction of the morally responsible 'subject'. Overpowered by the immoral force of noble being, the weak defend themselves by declaring that the strong are *responsible* for their actions which are now defined as freely willed, such that the strong could therefore act otherwise. Once slave morality has identified a subject behind and responsible for an action, that action may be reconfigured as the effect of a *moral decision*. This revaluation of values is complete when 'goodness' is redefined in moral terms as self-restraint in the interests of the weak. Nietzsche responds to this in characteristically scornful terms:

> A quantum of force is just such a quantum of drive, will, action, in fact it is nothing but this driving, willing and acting, and only the seduction of language (and the fundamental errors of reason petrified within it), which construes and misconstrues all actions as conditional upon an agency, a 'subject,' can make it appear otherwise. And just as the common people separates lightning from its flash and take the latter to be a *deed*, something performed by a subject, which is called lightning, popular morality separates strength from the manifestations of strength, as though there were an indifferent substratum behind the strong person which had the *freedom* to manifest strength or not. But there is no such substratum: there is no 'being' behind the deed, its effect and what becomes of it; the 'doer' is invented as an afterthought. . . .

> (2000: 28)

The invention of free will and the morally responsible subject enables weakness and impotence to be affirmed as positive moral virtues. Now it is *good* to lack the strength to determine one's own values and overcome outworn social structures. Morality is now judged from the perspective of the weak. This credo of self-sacrifice and world-renunciation is merely a cunning ploy, Nietzsche argues, because it is really the mechanism by which the weak impose their will and values on the world. The slavish man '*needs* to believe in an "unbiased" subject with freedom of choice, because he has an instinct of self-preservation and self-affirmation in which every lie is sanctified' (2000: 29). Nietzsche explores the revaluation of moral ideas by the weak in his critique of *ascetic values*.

ASCETIC VALUES

In historical terms, Nietzsche argues, the slave revolt in morals was propelled by the clerical caste (priests) and 'the Jews'. The Jews have a prominent place in this narrative because they were a people both dominated by priests and oppressed by hostile political conditions. The only way the Jews could alleviate their circumstances was by a 'radical revaluation' of moral values in which their exclusion from political authority was reinterpreted as the precondition for spiritual purity and strength (2000: 19). The term 'ascetic ideal' refers to this ethic of self-denial in which spiritual values are elevated above self-aggrandisement and worldly concerns. Fundamental to this slavish revaluation was the transformation of aristocratic rank or 'goodness' into *psychological* and *moral* superiority:

> It was the Jews who, rejecting the aristocratic value equation (good = noble = powerful = happy = blessed) ventured, with awe-inspiring consistency, to bring about a reversal and held it in the teeth of their unfathomable hatred (the hatred of the powerless), saying, 'Only those who suffer are good, only the poor, the powerless, the lowly are good; the suffering, the deprived, the sick, the ugly, are the only pious people, the only ones saved, salvation is for them alone, whereas you rich, the noble and powerful, you are eternally wicked, cruel, lustful, insatiate, godless, you will also be eternally wretched, cursed and damned!'
>
> (2000: 19)

Nietzsche's genealogy of moral history examines both the strengths and weakness of ascetic values. He begins by noting the *duplicity* of the ascetic renunciation of secular life in order to prepare the soul for the heavenly world to come. Far from renouncing power and secular authority, asceticism offers one of the most powerful techniques for imposing an interpretation on life. The will to self-denial is, after all, still an expression of *will*. It introduces a new economy of life in which cunning, self-consciousness and the transcendent idea of the 'soul' are privileged over strength, vitality, spontaneity and sensuality. The ascetic insists that hitherto mankind has suffered from a mistaken interpretation of life which can only be remedied if we accept his own 'valuation of existence' (2000: 90). Thus the priestly devaluation of sensuality, becoming and appearance is not merely a prelude to the apotheosis of spiritual truth but a manifestation of will to power by which the ascetic 'instinctively strives for an optimum of favourable conditions in which fully to release his power and achieve his maximum of power-sensation' (p. 81).

However, Nietzsche is not unequivocal in his condemnation of the slave revolt in morality. Whatever its shortcomings, the ascetic ideal furnishes mankind with a new mode of self-constitution and offers a new interpretation of life. Its reversal of 'familiar perspectives and valuations' enables us to experience new ideas and sensations so that we can 'use the *difference* in perspectives and affective interpretations for knowledge' (2000: 92). The production of the human 'soul' and the invention of 'evil' also gives mankind *depth* and adds an element of risk and danger to every moral decision. 'Man' is now distinguished from the rest of nature because he is the *interesting animal* (p. 18). The *paradox* of the ascetic ideal is that it constitutes a form of life *against* life – insofar as it systematically represses the spontaneous force of noble being – that also 'springs from the protective and healing instincts of a degenerating life which uses every means to maintain itself and struggles for its existence' (p. 93). The decline of aristocratic values meant that the ceaseless struggle and suffering of existence lacked meaning. The ascetic ideal filled this vacuum and 'offered man a meaning' (p. 127). It did so by arguing that life without divine redemption is meaningless; and *this* truth gives life its *meaning*. This revaluation of the meaning of suffering removed mankind's sense of 'suicidal nihilism' or the belief that life lacks all value (p. 127). The 'historic mission' of the priestly caste was to redirect the weak individual's reactive sense that someone *else* (the strong and the healthy) must be to blame for their unhappiness by *internalising* suffering and interpreting it according to the doctrine of guilt and original sin (p. 98). Now each of us becomes responsible for our own suffering; but if we subject existence to an ascetic interpretation (and subject ourselves to priestly authority) we may still be saved for the life to come.

While Nietzsche acknowledges the positive role the ascetic ideal has played in preserving degenerating life and saving mankind from nihilism, he consistently argues that it represents a form of life that must be *overcome*. The weakness of asceticism lies in its dependence upon a reactive reflex – the need for a form of being *beyond* the self ('God' or the 'soul') to define the self – in order to create and affirm values. Now 'goodness' means to be deprived of our own will and instinct and to give ourselves over to someone else's idea of truth. This revaluation means the sick can employ the rhetoric of divine 'justice' to repress the healthy and noble spirit in defiance of the pathos of distance that produces every powerful nature. The ascetic 'taste for moralization' reinforces this reversal by substituting fear of divine judgement for our unreflective and spontaneous vitality and imposing a religious interpretation on life (2000: 109). In this way it exploits 'the bad instincts of all sufferers for the purpose of self-discipline, self-surveillance and self-overcoming' (p. 100). Such self-overcoming, however, offers humanity no opportunity to determine its own values because the ascetic ideal 'inexorably interprets epochs, peoples, man, all with reference to this one goal, it permits of no other interpretation, no other goal, and rejects, denies, affirms, confirms only with reference to *its* interpretation' (p. 116).

The philosophical task Nietzsche presents himself is to offer humanity a path beyond the 'closed system of will, goal and interpretation' enforced by ascetic values (2000: 116). This task is imperative because asceticism, which saved humanity from the nihilistic horror of meaningless suffering, can ultimately bequeath only a *new* form of nihilism in its place. Despite its 'hatred' of the 'human' and its 'horror of the senses', asceticism originally provides a *will* to nothingness and a dynamic new interpretation of existence (p. 128). However, this ascetic interpretation is eventually challenged and overcome by a new will to truth that *denies* the authority of every religious and transcendental value. Ironically, this will to truth arises from *within* asceticism as that 'Christian conscience' which eventually develops into the 'objective truth' of scientific method. 'You see what it really was that triumphed over the Christian God', Nietzsche explains in *The Gay Science*, 'Christian morality itself, the concept of truthfulness that was understood ever more rigorously, the father confessor's refinement of the Christian conscience, translated and sublimated into a scientific conscience, into intellectual cleanliness at any price' (1974: 307). Unlike the thinking of Darwin (1809–82) and Freud, in which scientific truth is often seen as a rejection of religious premises, the ideal of scientific truth as seen by Nietzsche was an extension of the Christian will. Scientific conscience, he declares in the *Genealogy*, is 'the awe-inspiring *catastrophe* of a two-thousand year discipline in truth-telling, which finally forbids the *lie entailed in the belief in God*' (2000: 114). The nihilism of modern life is therefore produced by the overcoming of ascetic values by the will to truth of Christian morality itself:

> All great things bring about their own demise through an act of self-sublimation: that is the law of life, the law of *necessary* 'self-overcoming' in the essence of life. . . . In this way, Christianity *as a dogma* was destroyed by its own morality, in the same way Christianity *as a morality* must also be destroyed – we stand on the threshold of *this* occurrence. After Christian truthfulness has drawn one conclusion after another, it will finally draw the *strongest conclusion*, that *against* itself . . .
>
> (2000: 126–7)

NIHILISM

It is important to understand what Nietzsche means by 'nihilism' for two reasons. First, the concept is central to his examination of value and his critique of modernity. Secondly, 'nihilism' has gradually become detached from its place within Nietzsche's philosophy and established as a description of his work as a whole. Nietzsche is now routinely introduced to readers as a 'nihilistic' thinker in contexts where the term betokens a contempt for historical traditions and a refusal to endorse any particular moral or ethical position. While this popular representation draws upon elements of Nietzsche's critique of morality and modern politics, it also effaces the historical specificity of this critique and ignores its reflections upon the nature of a politics to come. To offer a proper account of Nietzsche's account of nihilism we need, instead, to understand its *double* character as both a historical diagnosis of the effects of slave morality and as a *transitional* movement towards a new era of aristocratic values.

This dual conception of nihilism as both a historical critique and the harbinger of a new style of living is underlined by Nietzsche's distinction between *active* and *passive* nihilism. He uses the term 'passive nihilism' to describe the life of moral decadence and *ressentiment* produced by slave morality and the decline of aristocratic values. In *The Will to Power*, Nietzsche remarks that passive nihilism represents 'the ultimate logical conclusion of our great values and ideals' — where 'great' is understood ironically to describe Christian ethics and the ascetic ideal (1968: 4). This conclusion is reached when the empirical 'truths' asserted by modern science dismiss divinity as a mythical illusion and render impossible the idea of a world of redemption in which weakness, humility and asceticism will be morally justified. The Christian-moral vision of a fallen world redeemed only by the transcendent life of the spirit was invented by mankind, Nietzsche argues, to ward off the perception that 'becoming has no goal and that underneath all becoming there is no grand unity in which the individual could immerse himself completely as in an element of supreme value' (p. 13). But once this vision is exposed as an illusion fabricated to meet 'psychological needs' we are denied the consolation of a transcendent world while lacking any belief in the value of our own existence. This is what passive nihilism means: humanity's 'highest' ideals *devaluate themselves* and it can create no new values to take their place:

> What has happened, at bottom? The feeling of valuelessness was reached with the realization that the overall character of existence may not be interpreted by means of the concept of 'aim', the concept of 'unity', or the concept of 'truth'. Existence has no goal or end; any comprehensive unity in the plurality of events is lacking: the character of existence is not 'true', is *false*. One simply lacks any reason for convincing oneself that there is a *true* world. Briefly: the categories 'aim', 'unity', 'being' which we used to project some value into this world – we *pull out* again; so the world looks *valueless*.

(1968:13)

Nietzsche takes the tendency to nihilism to its startling conclusion. If we *really* abandon belief in a higher world we must accept that '*every* belief, every considering-something-true, is necessarily false because there simply is no *true world*' (1986: 14). What we call the world is rather a ceaseless process of becoming within which different forms of life propagate themselves. It is therefore false to believe that we can be 'true' to the world or evaluate it in moral terms; the 'truth,' 'unity' and 'aim' of life are values that we impose on to the world in order to give our experience narrative coherence and meaning. The 'truth' of experience is, in these terms, indissociable from our will to truth and will to power:

> 'Truth' is therefore not something there, that might be found or discovered – but something that must be created and that gives a name to the process, or rather to a will to overcome that has in itself no end – introducing truth, as a *process in infinitum*, an active determining – not a becoming-conscious of something that is in itself firm and determined. It is a word for the 'will to power'.
>
> (1968: 298)

We create the truth of our experience by an 'active determining' of the process of becoming into a *version* of reality that cannot be discovered in the 'world itself'. This determination or fixing of the world varies according to the *perspective* from which we view it; it is only by privileging one perspective over another and creating a 'narrower, abbreviated, simplified world' that our experience can acquire meaning in the first place (1968: 15). The measure of our strength, Nietzsche argues, is defined by the 'extent we can admit to ourselves, without perishing, the merely *apparent* character' of the world and our constitutive role in projecting values upon it. This self-conscious emphasis upon the perspectival and creative character of our experience of the world has the potential to transform the nihilistic revelation of a world without an essential truth into a positive and rewarding event. For while the weak discover in this revelation only a feeling of worthlessness and loss, the strong individual acknowledges the merely apparent nature of experience in order to create a version of history that allows it to live productively and transform the world according to its own needs. This positive or *active* nihilism is a mode of existence that accepts our creative role in constituting the 'truth' of the world and the function of violence and force in promoting a strong and ascending form of life. Active nihilism is therefore a pivotal stage in the self-overcoming of 'man' and may well be '*a divine way of thinking*' (p. 15).

Two literary examples may illuminate Nietzsche's reflections on *ressentiment*, the creative constitution of truth and active nihilism. William Blake's prophetic work *The Marriage of Heaven and Hell* (1790) prefigured Nietzsche's work by suggesting that life is created and driven forward by force, struggle, disagreement and the radical expenditure of energy rather than the consensus of a generally accepted world view. Morality, in fact, is the residue left when the constant battle of contraries is rigidified into the religious and life-denying opposition of good and evil:

> Without contraries there is no progression. Attraction and repulsion, reason and energy, love and hate, are necessary to human existence.
>
> From these contraries spring what the religious call *good* and *evil*. Good is the passive that obeys Reason; Evil is the active springing from energy.
>
> Good is Heaven; Evil is Hell.
>
> (Blake 1989: 105)

Blake challenges the reactive restriction of energy and will into fixed moral dichotomies in two ways. His employment of enigmatic and seemingly contradictory aphorisms – 'Sooner murder an infant in its cradle than nurse unacted desires' – confronts the reader with a problem of interpretation and demonstrates that 'truth' is the singular perspective we impose on the world, not a shared and objective fact. Nietzsche later uses aphorisms in precisely the same way. Meanwhile the contrast Blake draws between the priest (who claims to *reveal* the meaning of existence by means of a division between body and soul, and man and God) and the poet-prophet (who *creates* values actively by force of will and imaginative energy) suggests that 'moral' thought is born at the moment we *forget* that humanity projects meaning imaginatively *on to* the world:

> The ancient poets animated all sensible objects with gods or geniuses, calling them by the names, and adorning them with the properties, of woods, rivers, mountains, lakes, cities, nations, and whatever their enlarged and numerous senses could perceive.
>
> And particularly they studied the genius of each city and country, placing it under its mental deity.
>
> Till a system was formed, which some took advantage of and enslaved the vulgar by attempting to realize or abstract the mental deities from their objects: thus began Priesthood, choosing forms of worship from poetic tales.

> And at length they pronounced that the gods had ordered such things.
> Thus men forgot that all deities reside in the human breast.
>
> (Blake 1989: 111)

In Blake's creation myth, the poets give life and meaning to the world. They do so by projecting their abundance of imagination and vitality outwards in the form of 'gods' or spirits who personify different qualities of life. Think, for example, of Aphrodite, goddess of love, and Mars, god of war. The poets also name the world, thereby lending it order and coherence. Forms of identity are conferred upon the earth, in order to perceive its flows and structures as 'woods, rivers, mountains, lakes, cities, nations'. However, this active and affirmatory *creation* of the world is repressed by the 'priests', who transform particular properties of existence like 'love' or 'strength' into general moral qualities to which all life must conform. It is the historical mission of the 'priests' to produce a uniform and moral interpretation of existence; this reinterpretation of life enslaves the weak by compelling them to subordinate their imagination to an inflexible moral law. Eventually, Blake suggests, the priestly reversal of cause and effect is taken to its logical conclusion: the gods are deemed themselves to be the creators of the world, rather then the expression of poetic inspiration, and the divine nature of the human imagination is forgotten.

The novel by the Algerian writer Albert Camus, *The Outsider* (of 1942), provides a celebrated example of active nihilism in the story of Meursault, a young French Algerian. Meursault creates an identity for himself wholly in opposition to established mores. He shares none of the 'humanistic' or 'moral' sentiments of the surrounding world: he feels no grief for his mother's death, treats the women he encounters with casual indifference, and remains unmoved by the prospect of advancement at work. In the central scene of the novel Meursault shoots and kills a young Arab who has been involved in a violent confrontation with his neighbour. During his trial and imprisonment he steadfastly refuses to 'account' for himself by embracing the 'moral' language of contemporary society or looking for salvation to a higher world. He recounts without comment the Prosecutor's claim that 'I didn't have one, a soul, and that I had no access to any humanity nor to any of the moral principles which protect the human heart' (2000: 98). Meursault refuses to justify himself because he believes that the only ethics of which humanity is capable is to take honest responsibility for one's own actions and not hide behind an abstract and empty moral code. The 'value' of our experience is to affirm our own actions. Everything that makes Meursault who he is led him to commit that murder; to attempt to find an extenuating circumstance for his actions would be to transform him into someone else. The world is indifferent to us; we project meaning on to it and must accept the consequences of the role we play within it. At least this is preferable, he argues, to the moral decadence of a society that sends priests to ask murderers to atone for their crimes while preparing them for the scaffold. Meursault's rupture with Christian morality leads to his final moment of affirmation:

> So close to death, mother must have felt liberated and ready to live her life again. No one, no one at all had any right to cry over her. And I too felt ready to live my life again. As if this great outburst of anger had purged all my ills, killed all my hopes, I looked up at the mass of signs and stars in the night sky and laid myself open for the first time to the benign indifference of the world. And finding it so much like myself, in fact so fraternal, I realised that I'd been happy, and that I was still happy. For the final consummation and for me to feel less lonely, my last wish was that there should be a crowd of spectators at my execution and that they should greet me with cries of hatred.
>
> (2000: 117)

For Nietzsche the active experience of nihilism has little to do with exhaustion of will or the renunciation of the world. It represents, instead, the catastrophic but *necessary* rupture with Christian morality required for a 'fruitful and powerful movement of humanity' to appear (1968: 69). 'It could be the sign of a crucial and most essential growth', Nietzsche suggests, 'of the transition to new conditions of existence, that the most extreme form of pessimism, genuine *nihilism*, would come into the world.' Nihilism provokes a crisis in mankind's relation to the world, but the value of this crisis is that it enforces a separation between strong and weak being and promotes an 'order of rank' by which a new aristocratic society may be created (p. 38). Only those who, like Nietzsche, have experienced this crisis have developed the strength of will to reject the illusion of a truthful world and a moral interpretation of existence. Thus while Nietzsche's conception of aristocratic or 'grand' politics exists to overcome nihilism as a way of life, the experience of nihilism as a moral crisis remains the indispensable point of transition that enables this new politics to be born.

GREAT POLITICS

Nietzsche's portrait of late nineteenth-century Europe is of a nihilistic culture that lacks the resources and self-confidence to overcome Christian morality and assert its own will to power. The causes of this decline are manifold: they include the triumph of slave morality and a politics of pity and *ressentiment*; the clamour of political democracy and equal rights which disdains the aristocratic order of rank; and general belief in a spurious scientific 'objectivity' or 'pure will-less knowledge' that is incapable of creating new values (1990a: 137). Nietzsche responds to this situation in *Beyond Good and Evil* by advocating the purification and redirection of the European 'will' by means of the development of a 'new caste' of elite beings (p. 138). The express function of this cultural elite is to overcome the exhausted example of Christian-moral 'man' and forge a world in its own image. 'The time for petty politics is past', Nietzsche declares; 'the very next century will bring with it the struggle for mastery over the whole earth – the *compulsion* to grand politics' (p. 138).

The revaluation of mankind can only be undertaken by a cultural elite because every 'elevation' of the type 'man' has 'hitherto been the work of an aristocratic society' (1990a: 192). Nietzsche's grand politics insists that the 'aristocracy' is the *'meaning* and supreme justification' of a society because it represents the most powerfully developed 'life-form' of which mankind is capable (p. 193). He uses the term 'aristocracy' to describe both an elite rank within society and an aesthetic of self-perfection which only the strongest individuals can sustain. A society declines, Nietzsche argues, when its aristocracy ceases to represent its highest type and is reduced to a mere *function* within it (as in the case of constitutional monarchy). Conversely, it is healthiest when organised hierarchically to produce a 'select species of being' (p. 193). The purpose of a grand politics is therefore the production of a higher type of 'man' and the 'breeding of a new ruling caste for Europe' (p. 183). Violence, force and the acceptance of the suffering of others is indispensable to its development; for mankind to overcome itself it must not 'yield to any humanitarian illusions: truth is hard' (p. 192). An aristocratic politics accepts with a 'good conscience' the 'sacrifice of innumerable men who *for its sake* have to be suppressed and reduced to imperfect men, to slaves and instruments' (p. 193). For every society that believes in a 'long scale' of orders and ranks, and establishes the noble pathos of distance, needs slavery and a slave caste to extend itself.

Nietzsche is unequivocal that violence and domination are fundamental to both the health of a noble society and to the development of a 'higher existence' (1990a: 193). An aristocratic society needs slavery 'in some sense' because the generation of a pathos of distance between master and slave produces 'ever higher, rarer, more remote, tenser, more comprehensive states' and a type of 'man' who can overcome morality and live beyond good and evil (p. 192). Only this elevated type can endure the burden of 'greatness' which demands extraordinary self-discipline and the continual transformation of weakness into new states of hardness and strength. Moreover, the concept of 'greatness' demands that we redefine the self in *aesthetic* terms as the quest for a form or style of living that gives coherent expression to our potential for self-perfection:

> In face of a world of 'modern ideas' which would like to banish everyone into a corner and 'speciality', a philosopher, assuming there could be philosophers today, would be compelled to see the greatness of man, the concept 'greatness', precisely in his spaciousness and multiplicity, in his wholeness in diversity: he would even determine value and rank according to how much and how many things one could endure and take upon oneself, how *far* one could extend one's responsibility.

(1990a: 143)

Nietzsche argues that his prospect of a style of living capable of embodying the aspirations of great politics is represented most forcefully by new *philosophers* like himself (1990a: 126). The 'new' philosopher is an exemplary case because the role of modern philosophy is to pose the meaning of the self as a *question* that might overcome the moral interpretation of life. He rejects the claim of timeless and foundational values and envisages the future of 'man' as 'his *will*', which prepares him for 'great enterprises and collective experiments in discipline and breeding so as to make an end of that gruesome dominion of chance and nonsense that has hitherto been called history' (p. 126). The new philosopher prepares mankind to overcome itself, for 'he comprehends in a *single* glance all that which, given a favourable accumulation and intensification of forces and tasks, could be *cultivated out of man*' (p. 127). Such preparation makes one overwhelming demand of 'man': it 'demands that he *creates values*' (p. 142). Mankind learns to create values for itself by following the example of the philosopher for whom self-legislation

and self-transformation is a law of life, and who possesses 'the conscience for the collective evolution of mankind' in an era of narrowness
and decadence (p. 86).

It is hardly surprising, given the violence of Nietzsche's rhetoric
concerning the ethical necessity of selective 'breeding', social exploitation and the production of a 'higher' type of 'man', that his name has
recurrently been associated with some of the most catastrophic events
of twentieth-century history. While his contempt for anti-Semitism and
the slavish veneration of a 'fatherland' demonstrate that he was very far
from the proto-Nazi whose imprimatur he bears in the popular imagination, his insistence upon the need for a slave class and his vagueness
about the ethical boundary between aristocratic self-restraint and the
necessary exploitation of the weak makes clear his own responsibility
for this interpretation of his work. However, a careful reading of
Nietzsche can reveal that his rhetoric of 'breeding' was anything but the
belief in a biological and already given master race. One could also argue
that Nietzsche confronted the language of nihilism – a language
grounded in mere life – and transformed it by envisaging 'breeding',
'selection' and aristocracy' in new, active and aesthetic terms.

In order to regain a sense of the complexity of Nietzschean politics
two points should be emphasised. First, Nietzsche's critique of social
democracy and equal rights does not equate the triumph of aristocratic
being with an exaltation of the 'individual'. On the contrary, he saw
the politics of individualism as a symptom of the herd instinct because
it claims that all individuals are *equally* valuable. Nietzsche's aristocratic
politics insists instead that 'what is right for one *cannot* by any means
therefore be right for another, that the demand for *one* morality for all
is detrimental to precisely the higher men, in short that there exists
an *order of rank* between man and man, consequently also between
morality and morality" (1990a: 158). The mark of aristocratic rank is
that it embraces life as will to power and envisages politics as the
creation of distinctions between higher and lower forms of being.
Nietzsche's aristocratic politics rebels constantly against the subordination of the being of 'man' to an abstract and general idea; this rebellion
explains his disdain for the 'lunacy of nationalism' and 'patriotic
palpitations and floods of various outmoded feelings' (pp. 188, 171).
Secondly, while it is true that he makes a distinction between the slavish
character of social democracy and what he saw as the necessary despotism of aristocratic politics, he viewed aristocratic despotism as the

inevitable historical *consequence* of the tyrannical nature of social democracy itself. Political democracy, he argued, embodies the inferior and slavish individual's tyrannical desire to invert noble values. Its legacy is the 'levelling and mediocritizing of man' and the elevation of the 'herd-animal' (p. 173). However, the lasting effect of the democratisation of Europe is to create both 'a type prepared for slavery' who need a master and the 'strong man' prepared to exploit the weak in order to express his own will to power. Nietzsche did not, then, imagine great politics to be simply the imposition of violence upon weakness but rather the replacement of one form of tyranny with another capable of promoting the values of an ascending mode of life.

Nietzschean 'great politics' has profound strengths and weaknesses. A principal strength of his aristocratic vision lies in its refusal to accept either an economic definition of individual worth or the utilitarian view that value is determined by the provision of the greatest happiness to the greatest number of people. To both the liberal demand for individual autonomy and the emancipatory claims of collectivist politics Nietzsche asked: What is meant by 'individualism' and who is it for? For Nietzsche the individual was a *practice*, not a mere political datum, which generated value by the cultivation of its will to power. This identification of value with power and will enabled him to discern the potentially regressive character of the will to power at the heart of egalitarian politics and offers a shrewd insight into the violence implicit in the goal of absolute equality. His sense of the fundamental inseparability of value and will to power also encouraged him to present the relation between past and present as creative and dynamic, and to place emphasis upon those aspects of our history that permit us to live productively now and in the future. Now historical value is defined by the selection and reproduction of our strongest and most creative capacities. As we will see, Nietzsche develops this connection between 'great' or higher life and will to power in his theory of the eternal recurrence.

Nevertheless, Nietzsche's great politics also leaves troubling questions in its wake. Is it possible to go 'beyond' morality (or good and evil) by moral exhortation? Why, in other words, *should* we follow Nietzsche's example? To what extent can politics escape making moral claims upon us (Ansell-Pearson 1994: 154)? How do we relate Nietzsche's immoral politics of domination to the idea of self-cultivation and restraint, and what marks the point of transition between the two? And is a *community* of new aristocratic philosophers really possible?

These questions haunt any discussion of Nietzsche's 'Overman', the prophetic figure who 'makes up for and redeems man, and enables us to retain our *faith in mankind*' (2000: 27). It is to this discussion we turn in the next chapter.

SUMMARY

Nietzsche continually links the question of the value of morality to his perception of the historical character of our moral values. He argues that the dichotomy of 'good' and 'evil' that organises moral reflection upon life does not reflect an eternal truth about the value of 'man'; it represents a historical reinterpretation of the pre-moral distinction between aristocratic and slavish nature. Morality is not an immutable aspect of human nature; it is a particular perspective upon life designed to elevate the interests of the weak and slavish over the strong and independent spirit. At the heart of this slave revolt in morals lies *ressentiment:* the creation of a reactive and moral vision of life wholly in opposition to aristocratic values. The ascendancy of slave morality throughout the last two thousand years has culminated in nihilism: a recognition of the exhaustion and bankruptcy of the slavish and Christian world view without any sense of what new evaluation of existence might take its place. Nietzsche's critique of morality claims that nihilism is both a spiritual and cultural crisis for humanity and the potentially positive sign of an impending rupture with slave morality, which promises the return of great politics and a vision of life beyond good and evil.

6

THE OVERMAN

This chapter examines two of Nietzsche's most important and controversial concepts: the 'Overman' (represented by the figure of Zarathustra) and the theory of the eternal recurrence. Nietzsche underlines the significance of these ideas to his work in his 'autobiography', *Ecce Homo*, first published in German in 1908. 'Within my writings my *Zarathustra* stands by itself', he recounts; 'I have with this book given mankind the greatest gift that has ever been given it' (1992: 5). The 'basic conception' behind the Overman, he continues, is 'the idea of the *eternal recurrence*, the highest formula of affirmation that can possibly be attained' (p. 69). The importance Nietzsche attached to these ideas is only rivalled, it seems, by the degree to which they have become misunderstood in the hundred years since his death. For Nietzsche's 'gift' of the Overman was quickly transformed into the nightmare vision of a fascistic 'Superman' who foreshadowed an inhuman and totalitarian world of rapacity and violence. Meanwhile the 'eternal recurrence' has long been caricatured as a weird cosmological doctrine preaching an empty fatalism – the theory that all moments of historical time recur continually in exactly the same order throughout eternity – that presents history as both endlessly dynamic and hopelessly static. The question therefore becomes: What did Nietzsche actually mean these ideas to represent and why did he envisage them as the culmination of a new vision for humanity?

Nietzsche introduces his conception of the Overman in *Thus Spoke Zarathustra*, first published in German in 1885. *Zarathustra* offers us a poetic and philosophical fable with a narrative completely different from all of his other books. It presents the experiences and teaching of the prophet Zarathustra who returns to civilisation after ten years of solitude, announces to mankind the death of God, and explains his vision of a life beyond supernatural values represented by the Overman. The lesson Zarathustra provides is that 'man' is a form of life that must be *overcome*. His narrative presents an epigrammatic and fragmentary account of an experience of being beyond the human and describes a series of encounters with men – even the 'highest' and 'ultimate' men – that suggest that mankind is a degenerate species that must find a new way of living. Zarathustra exists, in fact, as the symbol of Nietzsche's revaluation of all values and the exemplar of a higher type of being capable of existing beyond nihilism, *ressentiment* and the reactive values of slavish nature. His mode of being represents a transvaluation of 'man' and a new vision of what humanity might become. Such 'transvaluation' does not engage in moral argument by offering new and 'better' moral values; rather it looks at what values do and what form of life they promote.

It is important to recognise that the transvaluation represented by Zarathustra demands the overcoming of both nihilism and 'man' because Nietzsche argues that, far from appearing merely as a symptom of a declining form of life, nihilism constitutes the being of 'man' as he currently exists. Nietzsche's genealogy of morals argues that mankind comes into being through both active and reactive forces (noble natures reveal the ascendancy of the former and slavish natures the latter). However, the universal history of humanity reflects the gradual *conversion* of active forces into reactive states of being. Indeed, the very concept of the 'human' is reactive insofar as it posits an unchanging identity with which our values ought to accord. For this reason Nietzsche is consistently critical of the values of 'humanism', which lie at the core of modern western culture. Throughout his corpus Nietzsche repeats this melancholy story of reaction: it recurs in the destruction of Greek culture by 'theoretical' rationalism; the vanquishing of Roman values by Jewish piety; the reactive redefinition of Christian teaching by Saint Paul; and the decline of Napoleonic aristocracy into the modern culture of democratic ideas. The dilemma confronting mankind from the Greeks onwards, Nietzsche argues, it is that its active will has gradually

HUMANISM

Humanism is a relatively secular movement in both art history and the history of ideas. At the end of the Middle Ages, the Church began to lose its monopoly on thought and learning. Texts from ancient Greece and Rome were translated and reread. Of even greater significance was the development of the printing press, which allowed works of learning to be disseminated beyond the manuscript libraries of the monasteries. The key idea of humanism is that truth and value can be discerned by the human mind directly. Even if God exists, divine wisdom does not need to be revealed, mediated or interpreted by priests or the Church. By turning back to the ancient Greek philosophers, like Plato and Aristotle, and the Roman Stoics, like Seneca, humanists of the Renaissance affirmed the power of human reason to discover for itself the nature of truth. There was also an affirmation – in fine art and literature – of the beauty of human form, which was no longer seen as fallen and corrupt. A key example is Michelangelo's (1475–1564) representation of God as a human form reaching out to breathe life into a sensually depicted Adam whose body displays the divinity of creation. For Nietzsche, the seemingly secular appearance of humanism was a dangerous illusion. What appeared as a rejection of external authority – God, the priest and the Church – was not really a refusal of slavishness. Instead, 'man' is created in humanist culture as an ideal and moral norm and has a 'priest' internalised within him. The Overman, by contrast, embodies a life with enough power to live without stable norms and universal moral values.

become divorced from the power of affirmation that creates new values. Each of these victorious and reactive cultural periods emerges from an inversion of established values – democracy and equal rights are now seen as 'good' and the formation of an aristocratic elite as 'bad' – that leaves the underlying opposition between active and reactive forces firmly in place. What is needed instead, Zarathustra declares, is a mode of being that knows only affirmation and creates values from the experience of plenitude and strength. He dramatises this insight near the end of his narrative in the parable 'Of the Higher Men'.

Zarathustra's portrait of the 'Higher Men' develops Nietzsche's parody of the decadent and unexamined values that inform modern 'enlightened' thought. It begins by asking mankind's best representatives what the function and meaning of life should be in the wake of the scandalous news of the 'death of God' that Nietzsche announced in *The Gay Science*:

> The greatest recent event – that 'God is dead', that the belief in the Christian god has become unbelievable – is already beginning to cast its first shadows over Europe. For the few at least, whose eyes – the *suspicion* in whose eyes is strong and subtle enough for this spectacle, some sun seems to have set and some ancient and profound trust has been turned into doubt; to them our old world must appear daily more like evening, more mistrustful, stranger, 'older'. But in the main one may say: The event itself is far too great, too remote from the multitude's capacity for comprehension even for the tidings of it to be thought of having *arrived* as yet. Much less may one suppose that many people know as yet *what* this event really means – and how much must collapse now that this faith has been undermined because it was built upon this faith, propped up by it, grown in it; for example, the whole of our European morality. This long plenitude and sequence of breakdown, destruction, ruin, and cataclysm that is now impending – who could guess enough of it today to be compelled to play the teacher and advance proclaimer of this monstrous logic of terror, the prophet of a gloom and an eclipse of the sun whose like has probably never yet occurred on earth?
>
> (1974: 279)

The answer to the question posed by this passage is, of course, Zarathustra, whose role will be to transform 'terror' and 'gloom' into a new and positive vision of being. He is able so to do because he discerns in the death of God a profound possibility for the reawakening of life. The idea of God, Nietzsche contends, was the supreme achievement of *ressentiment* and reactive values: the invention of a 'higher' form of life in order to judge and condemn human will and earthly experience. Mankind clings to faith because it no longer feels able to create new values and styles of living. Faith is coveted most where will is lacking 'giving rise to a demand that has become utterly desperate for some "thou shalt"' (1974: 289). The metaphysical appeal to a transcendental or 'higher' world is indissociable from the flourishing of reactive forms and the preservation of declining life. This reactive gesture still persists when the being of God is denied: it may be discovered in systems of belief such as patriotism, positivistic science or revolutionary politics that identify absolute value outside the will of 'man' in abstract concepts like 'nation', 'the facts of nature' or 'universal rights'.

The challenge Zarathustra presents to the 'Higher Men' is to accept the responsibility of a life without God. It is natural, he argues, that the mob clings to the illusion of God because it confers a spurious equality upon mankind: ' "You Higher Men" – thus the mob blink – "there are no Higher Men, we are all equal, man is but man, before God – we are all equal!" ' (1969: 297). The Higher Men, however, have cast off their belief in God but lack the will to promote their own higher life in its place. Their weakness resembles Nietzsche's caricature of the English in *Twilight of the Idols*, first published in German in 1889, who 'have got rid of the Christian God, and now feel obliged to cling all the more to Christian morality' (1990b: 80). Thus while the Higher Men's mistrust of transcendental values marks a progression, they continually threaten to slide back into reactive attitudes. They have not yet 'suffered from *man*' and consequently their impulse is to preserve what is left of humanity rather than to impose a distinction between its ascending and descending forms of life (1969: 299). By preserving the strongest forces of a weak mode of existence the 'Higher Men' are in danger of producing a low type of being. Zarathustra outlines this gloomy diagnosis in his enigmatic remark that 'he who wants to be a first-born should see that he does not also become a last-born!' (1969: 302). The true passage beyond the empty and nihilistic humanism of Christian morality stripped of a Christian God is instead to embrace the overcoming of 'man' and the affirmation of will, great politics and the pathos of distance:

> Before God! But now this God has died! You Higher Men, this God was your greatest danger.
>
> Only since he has lain in his grave have you again been resurrected. Only now does the great noon-tide come, only now does the Higher Man become – lord and master! Have you understood this saying, O my brothers? Are you terrified: do your hearts fail? Does the abyss here yawn for you? Does the Hound of Hell yelp at you?
>
> Very Well! Come on you Higher Men! Only now does the mountain of mankind's future labour. God has died: now we desire – that the Superman shall live.
>
> (1969: 297)

READING THE OVERMAN

Nietzsche's choice of 'Zarathustra' as the prophet of a new experience of being is not arbitrary. For it was the Persian prophet Zoroaster (*c.* 630–*c.* 550 BC), according to Nietzsche, who first identified the moral struggle between good and evil at the heart of metaphysics and the universe. There is therefore an ironic justice in designating the originator of the 'error' of morality to overcome morality as such. 'The self-overcoming of morality throughout truthfulness, the self-overcoming of the moralist into his opposite,' Nietzsche explains, 'this is what the name Zarathustra means in my mouth' (1992: 98). This self-overcoming of man is exemplified by the 'Overman' (sometimes translated as 'Superman'). The term 'Overman' (Übermensch) carries two meanings crucial to Nietzsche's revaluation of values. 'Über' signifies 'over' in the sense of height and self-transformation: it suggests the elevation of mankind's highest self into an experience of being that has no trace of moralism or the fiction of free will. It can also suggest 'across' or 'beyond' and Nietzsche employs this second resonance to characterise 'man' as a bridge we must pass across toward a life free of *ressentiment* and negativity:

> But Zarathustra looked at the people and marvelled. Then he spoke thus:
> Man is a rope, fastened between animal and Superman – a rope over an abyss. A dangerous going-across, a dangerous wayfaring, a dangerous looking-back, a dangerous shuddering and staying-still.
> What is great in man is that he is a bridge and not a goal; what can be loved in man is that he is a *going-across* and a *going-down*.
>
> (1969: 43–4)

The transformation of 'man' into 'Overman' cannot take place without a 'going-down' or the destruction of man's reactive beliefs. The 'greatest thing' we can experience is 'the hour of the great contempt', when our ideas of happiness, reason, virtue, justice and pity appear to us as obstacles to our affirmation of our own will (1969: 42). These ideas are reactive because they are expressions of our own power that have become separated from life and reconfigured as a moral restraint upon our actions and attitudes. Zarathustra rails constantly against the transformation of active power into fixed concepts that judge and deny life. 'I entreat you, my brothers,' he cries, *'remain true to the earth,* and do not believe those who speak to you of superterrestrial hopes!' (p. 42). 'Superterrestrial' here refers both to 'God' and to any transcendent idea that separates mankind's active power from its immanent self-realisation. This injunction explains why 'man' is a bridge and *not* a goal. Those readings that envisage the Overman as the ultimate end or telos of mankind's evolutionary development merely compel each individual to conform to a general concept of 'man' and thereby reproduce the reactive elevation of an idea of life to judge life. Zarathustra satirises this presumption in his description of the 'Ultimate Man' whose claim to have discovered the meaning of existence leaves him weary of life and unable to experience active sensation and change (p. 46). In contrast, the Overman is not the 'end' of mankind but a *process* that transforms reactive values into the active affirmation of power.

A good example of what Nietzsche did *not* mean by the Overman appears in the character of Kurtz in Joseph Conrad's novella *Heart of Darkness* (1900). This may seem a surprising statement, because Kurtz is often understood to represent exactly the sort of challenge to the nihilism of modern culture that Nietzsche desired to provoke. *Heart of Darkness* presents a vision of the moral exhaustion of late nineteenth-century Europe reflected in the colonial appropriation of African resources. By this time, the pretence that European colonialism was defined by the Enlightenment ideal of a 'civilising mission' has long been revealed for what it always was: a desperate scramble for ivory, minerals and slaves. The journey of Conrad's protagonist Marlow, from the 'whited sepulchre' of Brussels to the chaos and horror of the Belgian Congo, exposes him to the corruption and systematic violence at the core of the colonial enterprise (Conrad 1989: 35). A French steamer pounds aimlessly at a deserted African beachhead while chained slaves lie starving in an abandoned clearing. All around him Marlow sees the devastating effect of the expression of superior power unconstrained by principle or purpose. This nightmarish spectacle represents, in Marlow's view, the collapse of colonialism into something far more sinister: 'robbery with violence' and 'aggravated murder' (p. 31). Colonialism, he argues, at least has an unsentimental 'idea' behind it: the self-overcoming of one culture by its expansion and appropriation of other spaces. As soon as this idea is abandoned for the unfettered pursuit of profit, colonialism degenerates into mere 'conquest', and chaos is loosed upon the world.

As Marlow's African odyssey develops, he hears repeatedly of one figure who seems to stand apart from the self-serving hypocrisy of the European colonial mission. Everywhere he goes word reaches him of Kurtz, the agent who suddenly tired of life at the colonial Central Station, and struck off on his own into the heart of the Congo. Kurtz leaves because he can no longer stomach the lie of colonialism that enables European traders to pretend that each colonial station 'should be like a beacon on the road toward better things, a centre for trade of course, but also for humanizing, improving, instructing' while they engage in mass murder for commercial gain (Conrad 1989: 65). It is, for Kurtz, simply weakness and self-deception to hide one's true motivation behind trite moralism and meaningless platitudes. Instead, the authentic response to the 'unearthly' and unfamiliar African landscape is to impose one's own will upon it without recourse to moral scruple or empty notions of Enlightenment (p. 69). Only in this way can we confront the inhuman 'truth' of the world with our own 'true stuff' and create our own laws and values.

Marlow is drawn initially to Kurtz's startling renunciation of established truths and values. Kurtz, he believes, 'kicked himself free of the earth' because he had the courage to abjure 'lies' and self-deceit about the meaning of his actions (Conrad 1989: 57). 'There is a taint of death, a flavour of mortality in lies,' Marlow reflects, 'which is exactly what I hate and detest in the world – what I want to forget.' But although Kurtz is strong enough to confront the 'wild and passionate uproar' of the African jungle, he remains too weak to lend these Dionysiac forces aesthetic shape and coherence; all he can do is visit violence, death and destruction upon the world around him (p. 69). In Zarathustra's terms, Kurtz lacks the restraint and self-awareness to transform reactive into active force and affirm a new interpretation of life. Kurtz can only experience the purely destructive aspect of the 'hour of the great contempt'; he is incapable of passing 'over' these reactive beliefs and ascribing a new meaning to life. In fact, life for Kurtz is reduced to pure negativity: the only vision he can finally articulate is 'the horror' of earthly existence (p. 111). Kurtz's fateful lack of restraint leads him to repeat the ultimate colonial fantasy: he sets himself up as an idol for the natives, who worship him with the rotting symbols of human sacrifice. His unwitting parody of the Overman is now complete: the inhuman force of life is reassimilated to the fixed concept of a god, and our prostration before transcendental illusions begins all over again.

Kurtz's fate in *Heart of Darkness* functions almost as a template of the vulgar interpretation of Nietzsche's philosophy of force and will. A careful reading of *Thus Spoke Zarathustra* demonstrates how distant this interpretation is from Nietzsche's own vision. Zarathustra encapsulates many of the key points of this vision in his discourse 'On the Blissful Islands'. The Blissful Islands disclose a landscape of natural beauty, harmony and abundance; they provide the perfect backdrop for Zarathustra's lesson that the meaning of human experience is to renounce transcendent illusions and remain true to the earth. Mankind should not worship God, Zarathustra argues, because it is unable to *create* a God. What we call 'God' is the type of reactive fantasy that appears whenever we project the truth of experience beyond the power of our 'creating will' (1969: 110). Mankind cannot conceive a God, but it can conceive the Overman by remaking the world in its own image and returning every transcendent idea to its proper basis in the human capacity for self-transformation:

> Could you *conceive* a god? – But may the will to truth mean this to you: that everything shall be transformed into the humanly-conceivable, the humanly-evident, the humanly-palpable! You should follow your own senses to this end!
> And you yourselves should create what you have hitherto called the World: the World should be formed in your image by your reason, your will, and your love! And truly, it will be to your happiness, you enlightened men!
>
> (1969: 110)

Every teaching that speaks of 'the one and the perfect and the unmoved and the sufficient and the intransitory' is 'evil and misanthropic' because it denies the human power of will and becoming through which mankind affirms itself by distinguishing between its active and reactive force (1969: 110). The value of mankind lies, instead, in its capacity to *overcome* its own reactive nature by a supreme act of will: 'Willing liberates: that is the true doctrine of will and freedom – thus Zarathustra teaches you' (p. 111).

The self-transformation of mankind can only be achieved once we acknowledge that seemingly absolute and timeless values such as 'good' and 'evil' were created by humanity to give existence a human meaning and to legitimate specific cultural and political arrangements. A 'value', Zarathustra reminds us, is a particular 'evaluation' of life created by those powerful enough to renounce established truths and to impose their perspective and needs upon others:

Truly, men have given themselves all their good and evil. Truly, they did not take it, they did not find it, it did not descend to them as a voice from heaven.

Man first implanted values into things to maintain himself – he created the meanings of things, a human meaning! Therefore he calls himself: 'Man', that is: the evaluator.

Evaluation is creation: hear it, you creative men! Valuating is itself the value and jewel of all valued things.

Only through evaluation is there value: and without evaluation the nut of existence would be hollow. Hear it, you creative men!

A change in values – that means a change in the creators of values. He who has to be a creator always has to destroy.

(1969: 85)

It requires strength to reject universal and timeless 'truths' like 'God' and to locate 'evaluation' and the creation of values at the heart of life. Zarathustra insists that the meaning of existence is determined by the *force* with which certain individuals seize hold of life and establish an interpretation of it. In order to overcome 'man' the Overman must develop a hard and martial nature and embrace the pitiless credo that 'what does not kill him makes him stronger' (1992: 11). Life is driven forward by risk, warfare and the overcoming of reactive forces; those who, like the 'last' or 'ultimate' man, have 'left the places where living is hard', can no longer provide an interpretation of life and drift list-lessly within a history they no longer control (1969: 46). In contrast, the Overman 'seizes the right to new values' by replacing every tradi-tional law or 'Thou shalt' with the affirmation of 'I will' (p. 55). This acceptance of the right and duty to create the meaning and value of the future distinguishes the Overman from the nihilistic men of *ressentiment* whose only wish is to 'will backwards' and punish those whose strength exceeds their own (p. 162). The Overman possesses the strength to create a law for itself which *cannot* be reduced to a general moral system or applied to the whole of humanity: 'I am a law only for my own,' Zarathustra cautions, 'I am not a law for all' (p. 296). The greatest act of self-affirmation is to give birth to one's own highest nature by purging oneself of nihilistic and reactive feelings (p. 301). Those who do so render themselves fit to share Zarathustra's virtues: they embody light-ness rather than the heaviness of *ressentiment;* they dance through time by affirming risk, chance and their difference from slavish nature; and their laughter finds its echo in Dionysius who teaches the necessity of destruction and self-transcendence in the furtherance of life:

If ever a breath of the creative breath has come to me, and a breath of that heavenly necessity that compels even chance to dance in star-rounds;

If ever I have laughed with the laugh of the creative lightning, which the thunder of the deed, grumbling but obedient, follows:

If ever I have played dice with the gods at their table, the earth, so that the earth trembled and broke open and streams of fire snorted forth:

For the earth is a table of the gods, and trembling with creative new words and the dice throws of the gods:

O how should I not lust for eternity and for the wedding ring of rings – the Ring of Recurrence!

(1969: 245)

ETERNAL RECURRENCE

The description above of Zarathustra's virtues concludes with a reference to 'Eternal Recurrence', which Nietzsche describes as 'my real idea from the abyss' and absolutely crucial to his thought (1992: 11). This 'idea' has proved endlessly controversial in philosophical circles and has spawned radically different interpretations. Nietzsche offers a tantalising clue to his meaning in a sentence in *Ecce Homo* which is extended by a passage from Zarathustra's parable 'Of Redemption':

On one occasion Zarathustra strictly defines his task – it is also mine – the *meaning* of which cannot be misunderstood: he is *affirmative* to the point of justifying, of redeeming even the entire past:

I walk among man as among fragments of the future: of that future which I scan.

And it is all my art and aim to compose into one and bring together what is fragment and riddle and dreadful chance.

And how could I endure to be a man, if man were not also poet and reader of riddles and the redeemer of chance!

To *redeem the past* and to transform every 'It was' into an 'I wanted it thus!' – that alone would I call redemption.

(1992: 80)

The eternal recurrence, it seems, is inseparable from a philosophy of will – transforming 'it was' into 'I wanted it thus' – that promises a radically revised relationship between past and present and a new art of living. It is difficult absolutely to adjudicate this claim because

Nietzsche's stylistic (and philosophical) tendency to scatter his remarks across several texts without synthesising them into a uniform perspective presents formidable problems of interpretation. Perhaps the clearest way to introduce the idea of eternal recurrence is to suggest two perspectives, which supplement one another: an *existential* reading (which considers it within the ethical context of how the strong individual ought to live) and a *cosmological* reading (which presents an inhuman perspective from which to consider human experience as a whole). Nietzsche provides the existential context for eternal recurrence in a famous section from *The Gay Science:*

> What if some day or night a demon were to steal after you into your loneliest loneliness and say to you: 'This life as you now live it and have lived it, you will have to live once more and innumerable times more; and there will be nothing new in it, but every pain and every joy and every thought and sigh and everything unutterably small or great in your life will have to return to you, all in the same succession and sequence – even this spider and this moonlight between the trees, and even this moment and I myself. The eternal hourglass of existence is turned upside down again and again, and you with it, speck of dust!'
>
> Would you not throw yourself down and gnash your teeth and curse the demon who spoke thus? Or have you once experienced a tremendous moment when you would have answered him: 'You are a god and never have I heard anything more divine.' If this thought gained possession of you, it would change you as you are or perhaps crush you. The question in each and every thing, 'Do you desire this once more and innumerable times more?' would lie upon your actions as the greatest weight. Or how well disposed would you have to become to yourself and to life to *crave nothing more fervently* than this ultimate eternal confirmation and seal?

(1974: 273–4)

The question posed to humanity by the demon appears to be an existential challenge of commitment and engagement: In what way would you have to live your life so that the joy of existence would justify even the most terrible and painful events? This challenge leads in turn to other questions. Do you have the courage to affirm your style of living if each moment, good and bad, were to return eternally? What would you need to change in your life to produce such an affirmation? And could you affirm a life that accepted suffering, pain and hardship as the condition for self-overcoming and a new vision of 'man'? It is crucial to recognise that Nietzsche is writing in the conditional mood ('What if') because this passage confronts its reader with the promise (and the peril) of becoming and change. Could we accept the prospect of eternal recurrence if it were extended to us, Nietzsche wonders, or would we have to reject it because we lived reactively and in the spirit of *ressentiment*? And are we able to accept this earthly life without the transcendent hope of God, redemption or the prospect of another life to come?

Nietzsche develops his reflection upon recurrence in Zarathustra's parables of 'The Convalescent' and 'The Intoxicated Song'. In the first Zarathustra is awoken by the most 'abysmal thought' – the revelation of the 'circle' of life – and slips into a coma for seven days (1969: 233). His collapse is a consequence of his disgust with mankind: he dreamed that man had crept into his throat and choked him. Such disgust may only be overcome, Nietzsche suggests, if Zarathustra and mankind have the strength to change their lives. He therefore uses the narrative of 'The Convalescent' (a title that refers to Zarathustra and potentially to humanity as a whole) to create an ethical distinction between two different attitudes towards recurrence. On one side is Zarathustra, who is forced to confront the unpalatable fact that eternal recurrence applies even to the 'smallest' and most reactive man rather than consisting simply in the affirmation of the highest natures (1969: 236). Paradoxically, however, the self-conscious affirmation of the return of even reactive natures produces the aristocratic distinctions Zarathustra is so anxious to preserve. For only the noblest nature can experience the endless cycle of destruction and creation for itself and affirm its inescapable and constitutive relationship with everything it despises. In contrast, Zarathustra's animals can only repeat his new 'doctrine' without accepting the demon's challenge and considering its consequences for their *own* lives. Yet without self-consciousness there is, for Zarathustra, no ethical affirmation and he recoils in disgust at the 'hurdy-gurdy song' his creatures have made of his experience (1969: 235).

Why, however, should it be necessary for *all* things to return in order to effect our *own* individual recurrence? The answer lies in Nietzsche's critique of the subject and his creation of a philosophy of forces. Nietzsche, we remember, consistently denied the existence of a substantial being behind the multiplicity of actions and reactions that constitute life. Thus there is nothing behind my actions – such as a 'subject' or 'soul' – that orders their distribution and gives them meaning. We are what we do; each of us 'is' the experiences we have and the impressions our force registers on other objects. If our being is not constituted by an irreducible essence but arises instead from our position within a cosmic network of forces, actions and reactions, it is necessary for *everything* to return as it was for our being to reproduce itself. As soon as a single force or action is changed the universe is altered ever so slightly and everything within it mutates into something else. The strong nature is able to affirm its location within a network of forces and will the return of every force, whether its effect be malign or ennobling. To affirm the eternal recurrence of every force is to affirm and redeem the world now – rather than in a metaphysical hereafter – and enables us to eternally become who we are. The being capable of such affirmation exhibits Nietzsche's 'formula for greatness in a human being', namely *amor fati* (love of fate) or the belief that 'one wants nothing to be other than it is, not in the future, not in the past, not in all eternity' (1992: 37). Zarathustra encapsulates this belief in his claim that 'the time has passed when accidents could befall me; and what *could* still come to me that was not already my own?' (1969: 173). It reappears as the template of his philosophy of affirmation and joy in 'The Intoxicated Song':

> Did you ever say Yes to one joy? O my friends, then you said Yes to *all* woe as well. All things are chained and entwined together, all things are in love;
>
> If ever you wanted one moment twice, if ever you said: 'You please me, happiness, instant, moment!' then you wanted *everything* to return!
>
> You wanted everything anew, everything eternal, everything chained, entwined together, everything in love, O that is how you *loved* the world,
>
> You everlasting men, loved it eternally, and for all time: and you say even to woe: 'Go, but return!' *For all joy wants – eternity!*
>
> (1969: 331–2)

Nietzsche's remarks on eternal recurrence have been somewhat obscured by the controversy surrounding his insistence that recurrence is not merely an existential challenge – the question of how to live – but a cosmological truth or a theory of the world. In several sections of his working notes (posthumously published as *The Will To Power*) he claims that the recurrence of all things is the fundamental dynamic of the universe and 'the most *scientific* of all possible hypotheses' (1968: 36). He seeks to establish his cosmological thesis in the proposition that the universe cannot be thought to be progressing towards an end or goal because this goal would already have been reached:

> If the world could in any way become rigid, dry, dead, *nothing*, or if it could reach a state of equilibrium, or if it had any kind of goal that involved duration, immutability, the once-and-for-all (in short, speaking metaphysically: if becoming *could* resolve itself into being or into nothingness), then this state must have been reached.

> (1968: 548–9)

Nietzsche's position may be summarily stated: if we accept that both space and cosmic forces are finite ('If the world may be thought of as a certain definite quality of force and as a certain definite numbers of centers of force . . .'), and also that an eternity may already have passed between the unspecified origin of time and the present moment, it follows that the world must pass through 'a calculable number of combinations' of events (1968: 549). Under these conditions, the very possibility of infinite time means that 'every possible combination would at some time or another be realized; more: it would be realized an infinite number of times' (p. 549). We can arrive at the same destination by another route. If time had a beginning, Nietzsche argues, there would necessarily be some point before time. This makes no sense. But if time has no beginning then life is eternal. If life is eternal then we cannot see the present as a point from which time moves forward (for what would it be moving from?). Eternity has already taken place. Now, if time has no boundary there is no beginning or end, no point before or after time. Everything is as it will always be: a flux without direction or outside. As Zarathustra exults at one point, 'For me – how could there be an outside-of-me? There is no outside!' (1969: 234). Eternal recurrence therefore becomes the fundamental principle of being.

Nietzsche's cosmological thesis has since proved vulnerable to developments in quantum physics and new models of probability theory. Many commentators have rejected 'eternal recurrence' as a philosophical oddity on the basis of these objections. However, if we look beyond the 'scientific' implications (or otherwise) of Nietzsche's remarks and try to establish why he propounded them so forcefully, two ideas emerge that reinforce the idea of recurrence as an existential challenge: the vision of a non-teleological experience of life and a philosophy of force and affirmation. The persistent motif of Nietzsche's discussion of recurrence as 'existence as it is, without meaning or aim, yet recurring inevitably without any finale of nothingness' is its resistance to the idea that life has a purpose and tends towards a final goal or that the meaning of existence is to be found in the causal relations of human experience (1968: 35). There can be no ultimate goal of life if all events recur eternally; the thought of recurrence begins at the point where mankind 'ceases to *flow out* into a god' and affirms the power and plenitude of being in every lived moment (1974: 230). The vision of eternal return without end or goal is not meant to abandon us to the brute power of anonymous cosmic laws; Nietzsche conceives eternal recurrence in part as a critique of 'mechanism', which identifies the origins of life in the 'attraction and repulsion' of impersonal material forces (1968: 333). The thought of recurrence demands, instead, that we ascribe an 'inner will' to universal forces by *choosing* which returning moments we wish to affirm and using them to offer a new interpretation of life. To think of 'laws' of nature without thinking also of the will that orders them into hierarchies of value is to condemn ourselves to an empty fatalism. Conversely, Nietzsche argues that the 'unalterable sequence of certain phenomena' always demonstrates 'a power relationship between two or more forces' because historical events only acquire their meaning when they are shaped into coherence by a strong will (1968: 336). This is why the Overman embodies the principle of eternal return: he affirms the difference of what returns by giving each event its particular significance and making it his own.

The enigmatic notion of eternal recurrence can be illuminated by reference to a Hollywood film: Harold Ramis's *Groundhog Day* (1993). Nietzsche, we recall, argued that one of the chief causes of nihilism was our tendency to project an ultimate value or end beyond life in the form of heaven, the promise of redemption or the prospect of happiness to come. We therefore devalue life in order to transcend life. The challenge Nietzsche poses to this nihilistic devaluation is to ask: What if there were only this life with no outside or beyond, lived as eternal recurrence? Could we affirm such a life and, by so doing, renounce transcendental values and the dream of a future life?

The questions are explored comically in *Groundhog Day*. Its protagonist, television weatherman Phil Connors, can find no value in life and affects a cynical and world-weary boredom with existence. Every day is the same, every weather report resembles the one before, and his social relationships end in failure and recrimination. Connors's nihilistic disdain for life is exacerbated when he is sent by his television station to Punxsutawney, Philadelphia, in order to report upon the annual Groundhog Day celebrations. A blizzard sweeps into town, cutting it off from the outside world, and leaving Connors trapped in the type of provincial rural community for which he reserves his most blistering scorn. Worse is to follow. When Connors wakes the next morning, he discovers that he appears condemned to live out the previous day all over again. Everything is the same: the radio reports, the weather, the gestures and the comments of the people he meets. And every subsequent day merely repeats the same pattern all over again. This is Connors's fate: to be trapped in a cycle of eternal recurrence in what he takes to be the worst place on earth: Punxsutawney, Philadelphia.

The comedy and the pathos of *Groundhog Day* inhere in Connors's response to his extraordinary situation. At first, he is bewildered and horrified by this new course of events, which simply confirm his nihilistic devaluation of existence. He falls into despair, and tries desperately to escape his life, by either destroying or denying the present. Everything bores him, his jokes stale quickly, and he sees no point or value in life. Existence becomes worthless to him precisely because it appears to him as perpetually the same. Connors's nihilistic despair culminates in a series of suicide attempts, but the tragi-comic nature of his dilemma permits him no exits. After every 'death', he awakens again the next morning, and his day unfolds as before.

However, Connors's entrapment within an endless recurrence of experience also opens him up to a new perspective upon life. He gradually comes to understand that if there is *just* the endless recurrence of this life then the repetition of the same leads to an infinite experience of *difference*. All things become possible because instead of being confined within a differentiated personal life, we could live each day as one more moment in an *eternal* and impersonal becoming. Each of us could live through every event, adopt multiple personae and become all persons. Connors's life begins comically to express this radical potential: he becomes a jazz pianist, virtuoso ice-sculptor and an expert in French symbolist poetry. Moreover, his recognition that life is an eternal movement of becoming rather than a purposive narrative with a beginning, middle and end leads him to select the ascending forces of his own life and to reject self-pity, nihilism and *ressentiment*.

Connors's radical experience of recurrence is ultimately at odds with the broader ideological interests of both the film and the Hollywood system. The final stages of *Groundhog Day* retreat from its main theme by returning its audience to a secure sense of bourgeois moral values. Life, its conclusion reassures us, does have a purpose and end: finding love and marrying the girl of your dreams. But despite this reactive return to a specific, located and familiar set of values, it is the capacity of the thought of recurrence to present morality as a problem that enables the film's comic vision to resonate beyond its generic parameters.

SUMMARY

The Overman represents a creative and affirmative vision of life beyond the negativity of nihilism, *ressentiment* and slave morality. His teaching seeks to overcome the nihilistic experience of life produced by the 'death of God' and to affirm a new interpretation of existence without recourse to supernatural values. This new interpretation of life envisages a new mode of being that knows only affirmation and creates values from the superabundance of will, plenitude and strength. To affirm existence from this perspective is to overcome the reactive vision of 'man' and the mystification of a 'higher' world and to enforce a distinction between ascending and descending forms of life. The Overman reinforces this active reinterpretation of life by his teaching of eternal recurrence. Recurrence presents both an existential and a cosmological justification of our experience. It describes a non-teleological vision of life and a philosophy of force and affirmation. The strong individual is able to embrace the inevitable and eternal return of all his past experiences – both good and bad – because he has the power to choose which of these experiences he wishes to affirm and thereby create a new interpretation of life beyond every moral and reactive evaluation.

7

THE WILL TO POWER

This chapter examines one of Nietzsche's most important and enigmatic formulations: will to power. Of all of Nietzsche's terms, 'will to power' is the one most closely associated with his name in the popular imagination, where it is generally taken to describe a vision and a justification of life conceived as the violent domination of the weak by the strong. Like most clichés, this reading conceals a residue of truth, but it only highlights the most dramatic element of what Nietzsche claims to be an entirely new theory of life. In anticipation of the difficulties that beset discussions of this field, it must be said that it is uncertain whether 'will to power' may even be adequately represented as a 'theory', 'idea' or 'principle' given Nietzsche's insistence that it names a productive force that both creates and transforms any version of 'being' or 'reality' that we encounter. The world envisaged as will to power, we might say, offers a *dynamic* vision of life experienced simultaneously as noun and verb in which every aspect of existence receives a new interpretation. In order to understand this new vision of life, however, we must first determine what Nietzsche meant by 'will' and 'power' and establish exactly what is at stake in rethinking life in these terms.

The primary importance to Nietzsche of 'will to power' is that it offers him a radically new perspective on the challenges and paradoxes that his work generated. Nietzsche's attempt to develop a critical position 'outside' the reactive and nihilistic history of western thought confronted him with a series of contradictions. How is it possible to write a *history* showing the corrupt formation of man as a 'historical' animal? How can you *argue* for the spurious nature of reasoning? Is it possible to insist on the *falsity* of truth? All these questions led Nietzsche to reconsider the nature of life and its capacity to produce 'man' as a being of paradox and contradiction. This revisionary process eventually led him to challenge some of the fundamental dualisms – such as the oppositions between appearance and reality or being and becoming – that underpinned his early work. He suggested, instead, that any attempt to think what is 'outside' a notion of truth only becomes one *more* version of truth. Any rejection of 'man' creates merely one more human norm: 'Act in such a way that you are opposed to every humanist conception of life.' The conception of 'will to power' represented to Nietzsche the possibility of moving beyond the contradictions imposed by critical thought by conceiving a principle of life *interior* to life, rather than occupying a critical position above and beyond life in the form of transcendental reason. An *immanent* principle – accepting nothing more than life – would enable us to see how the divisions between different forms of life (animal life, physiological life, rational life, moral life and so on) were produced and legitimated. Nietzsche argued that we need to see all life, not just human life, as united by a common striving for power. Human life (with all its truths and norms) is merely a form through which life *passes*.

Nietzsche's commitment to developing a new vision of existence originates, then, in his recognition that western reflection upon life has traditionally been structured by the metaphysical opposition between a number of fixed terms. The most significant of these oppositions are between subject and object, cause and effect, and being and becoming. Nietzsche argued that this dualistic tendency in western thought is entrenched within, and produced by, the structure of the language we use to represent the world. We are reminded here of Nietzsche's famous aphorism in *Twilight of the Idols* that 'we are not getting rid of God because we still believe in grammar' because it underlines his conviction that our perception of the world is dependent upon the linguistic division between different forms of life (1990b: 48). Grammar functions, after all, by enforcing a distinction between a 'subject' (often represented by the human consciousness or 'man') and an 'object' (the external world). This distinction is extended further by grammatical ideas like 'verbs', 'nouns' and 'adjectives', which encourage us to perceive movement and change as experiences that happen *to*, rather than create, a human subject, and that transform the world from an endless process of becoming into an oscillation between relatively determinate states, actions and experiences.

The standard metaphysical imposition of a world of form and substance over a world of becoming and change is reinforced, Nietzsche argues, by the belief in a faculty of reason that mistakenly posits self-consciousness as the fundamental quality of being and then projects this belief in an 'ego-substance' on to the world in general. By means of this transposition the human 'ego' and 'will' are envisaged as the origin and cause of existence rather than as a secondary *effect* of a more general and inhuman movement of life. The being of the world is therefore represented in merely human terms. To live today is to be

> entangled in error, *necessitated* to error, to precisely the extent that our preju-
> dice in favour of reason compels us to posit unity, identity, duration, substance,
> cause, materiality, being ... Language belongs in its origin to the age of the
> most rudimentary form of psychology: we find ourselves in the midst of a rude
> fetishism when we call to mind the basic presuppositions of the metaphysics
> of language – which is to say, of *reason*. It is *this* which sees everywhere deed
> and doer; this which believes in will as cause in general; this which believes in
> the 'ego', in the ego as being, in the ego as substance, and which *projects* its
> belief in the ego-substance on to all things – only thus does it *create* the concept
> 'thing'. . . . Being is everywhere thought in, *foisted on*, as cause: it is only from
> the conception 'ego' that there follows, derivatively, the concept 'being'. . . . At
> the beginning stands the great fateful error that the will is something which
> *produces an effect* – that the will is a *faculty*. . . . Today we know it is merely
> a word.
>
> (1990b: 47–8)

Nietzsche's elaboration of the 'will to power' attempts to free us from the error of representing existence in merely anthropomorphic terms by conceiving of an *inhuman* principle of creation that both *constitutes* and *exceeds* human life. This sense of life as a ceaseless and inhuman struggle for power and dominion helps explain Nietzsche's unwillingness – puzzling to many readers – to discuss 'will' in psychological and human terms. He refuses to identify will with consciousness because the latter introduces a false causality into events by taking a set of effects (thoughts, feelings and the contents of our inner life) to be the origin of our sensible experience of the world. The mistake we make is to imagine that conscious ideas like 'pleasure' and 'pain' are the cause of bodily reactions and that the maximisation of pleasure and the avoidance of pain are the motives for every kind of action. For Nietzsche, however, these ideas begin as *interpretations* of material physical processes. He offers both a physiological and an historical justification of this claim. Thus he argues in *The Will To Power* that a rush of blood to the head and a change in our pulse and breathing is commonly interpreted as 'anger', while this feeling actually originates in a physiological movement that has little to do with conscious intention (1968: 354). Eventually we become so habituated to associating certain external incidents (such as people, places and things) with particular feelings that we assume them to be the cause of physiological change. Elsewhere the briefest recourse to the history of human sexuality and taste demonstrates that what constitutes 'pleasure' and 'pain' is determined by particular cultural judgements rather than a general biological law. A practice like sadomasochism suggests that pain may be interpreted as the precondition and apotheosis of pleasure rather than its absolute antithesis. Meanwhile, the development of spiritual asceticism reveals a physiological intensity and ecstasy in privation that reproduces the effect of sexual pleasure while enabling a moral condemnation of carnal indulgence. Pleasure and pain are not therefore simply psychological causes of physical change. They are retrospective judgements placed upon physiological processes whose meaning varies according to the feeling of power they make possible in the subject experiencing them (p. 354).

To judge life in terms of its conformity to certain conscious ideas – pleasure and displeasure, for example, or good and evil – demands that we transform an effect of life into its cause and ultimate justification. Nietzsche declares repeatedly that consciousness is, in fact, a *secondary* and *reactive* form of being that lies initially 'at the furthest distance from the biological center of the individual', until a gradual process of 'becoming conscious' posits conscious ideas as the cause of physiological sensations (1968: 274). He describes consciousness in biological terms merely as something 'added' to the nervous system that introduces a principle of causation into life where none is otherwise discernible, in order to make the world humanly *thinkable* (p. 285). This process substitutes a self-reflective 'unity' for the 'thousandfold complexity' of life and elevates the sovereign consciousness of 'man' into the highest value of existence (p. 284). However, becoming conscious is only one *more* means towards the unfolding and extension of the power of life; understanding life primarily in conscious terms denies the *multiplicity* of ways life realises and extends itself (p. 376). To posit an idea like pleasure, morality or spirituality as the highest value of existence is to deny the total economy of life and take a part for the whole of nature. Moreover, the identification of the sphere of consciousness as an unconditional value behind life to explain life replicates the naive belief in an absolute spirit or 'God' that was the supreme achievement of reactive thought:

> The fundamental mistake is simply that, instead of understanding consciousness as a tool and particular aspect of the total life, we posit it as the standard and condition of life that is of supreme value: it is the erroneous perspective of *a parte ad totum* [from a part to the whole] – which is why all philosophers are instinctively trying to imagine a total consciousness, a consciousness involved in all life and will, in all that occurs, a 'spirit', 'God'. But one has to tell them that precisely this turns life into a monstrosity; that a 'God' and total sensorium would altogether be something on account of which life would have to be condemned – Precisely because we have *eliminated* the total consciousness that posited ends and means, is our great relief – with that we are no longer *compelled* to be pessimists – *Our* greatest *reproach* against existence was the *existence of God*.
>
> (1968: 376–7)

WILL, POWER AND RESISTANCE

Nietzsche's negative critique of consciousness and spirit as the highest value of existence prepares us for his *positive* vision of life. This vision is shaped by three principal convictions. First, the whole of life is a single field of forces created by an inhuman will to power, which produces human consciousness as one of its effects. What we call 'life' is a ceaseless force of becoming and transformation which our linguistic conventions habitually divide into a cause and an effect. Second, the aim of life is neither self-preservation nor moral and spiritual enlightenment but the *increase of power* and 'the will to appropriate, dominate, increase, grow stronger' (1968: 367). Mankind's history, he notes, offers countless examples of individuals risking their lives in pursuit of power and dominion. The fundamental life-drive consists in the accumulation of force and the overcoming of resistance manifested when a stronger dominates a weaker will. This relationship of power characterises every stage of life: it is present, of course, in physical acts of subjugation; but it is also the motive force behind intellectual forms such as philosophical dialogue or the ritual conventions of courtly love as well as what shapes the historical modulation between emerging and declining cultural movements.

This monist vision of one single force or principle underlying being led Nietzsche to argue that there is absolutely no other kind of causality than the movement of domination between one will and another (1968: 347). For this reason 'will' must be rigorously detached from abstract psychological categories like 'desiring' or 'demanding', which place a conscious *idea* before the expenditure of force. There is no such thing as 'willing', Nietzsche declares: there is only willing *something* (p. 353). The entire movement of life is produced by the conflict between the will to the accumulation of force and that which resists incorporation into a stronger will. This conflict between appropriation and resistance informs every level of life and produces the distinctions that differentiate one level from another: the question at stake in every 'event' of life, Nietzsche asserted, is 'the degree of resistance and the degree of superior power' (p. 337). What he calls a 'quantum' of will to power – the extent to which a superior power can assimilate an inferior force to itself – is the productive unit of life that 'cannot be thought out of the mechanistic order without taking away this order itself' (p. 338). The growth of a species and the measure of its desire for knowledge depends therefore upon the extent to which it masters and extends its will to power. In a stunning reversal, Nietzsche claims that knowledge is an *effect* of power rather than its precondition; we become 'knowledgeable' insofar as we possess the power to create a vision of reality and impose this vision upon others (p. 267). Similarly, our conscious ideas of 'pleasure' and 'displeasure' are not causes of action but the consciousness of *difference* between the level of power we once embodied and the level we own now (p. 366). To feel pleasure is to feel the maximisation of force, while displeasure marks the redirection of a weaker by a stronger will:

> The will to power can manifest itself only against resistances; therefore it seeks that which resists it – this is the primeval tendency of the protoplasm when it extends pseudopodia (protrusion of protoplasm from a cell for feeding) and feels about. Appropriation and assimilation are above all a desire to overwhelm,

> a forming, shaping and reshaping, until at length that which has been over-
> whelmed has entirely gone over into the power domain of the aggressor and
> has increased the same.
>
> (1968: 346)

The third element of Nietzsche's philosophy of will is that will to power *interprets* by identifying a hierarchy of force between different forms of life. By 'interpretation' Nietzsche means a way of becoming *master* of something: will to power interprets by defining limits between types of being, assessing the degree of force exhibited by each type, and determining the extent to which one being has successfully assimilated another to its domain (1968: 342). Because will to power is the productive force that constitutes every level of life, interpretation understood in the Nietzschean sense is fundamental to the experience of being. Nietzsche regularly reinforces this point in order to expose the deformation of our view of the world by the fiction of subjective 'purpose' and 'intention'. He argues that it is inadequate to look for the meaning of an action in an intentional 'purpose' because 'purpose and means are interpretations whereby certain points in an event are emphasized and selected at the expense of other points' (p. 351). We should refrain from endorsing the fiction of a 'subject' and projecting a 'doer' into every deed because once we give up the 'effective subject' we also dispense with the ground upon which a range of conceptual falsifications – such as the belief in a primary 'substance' of being with 'essential' and 'accidental' attributes or the idea of a 'thing-in-itself' – are produced (p. 298). We cling tenaciously to the idea of the self-identical subject because it provides a stable and singular perspective from which the multiplicity of life may be ordered into coherence. Once the 'truth' and 'substantiality' of the 'real' has been established, it becomes possible to enforce a division between the integrity of a world-in-itself and a fraudulent world of 'appearance' that privileges the metaphysical and reactive forms of the 'soul' and the 'ego' over the corporeal world of becoming. This division is menaced as soon as the subject and the 'real' are exposed as effects of a mobile force of accumulation and resistance, the boundaries of which are constantly being reconfigured. Nietzsche rejects the *substantial* difference between subject and object; the subject emerges from a world of difference, in which the flux of atoms has no pre-given essence:

No subject 'atoms'. The sphere of a subject constantly growing or decreasing, the center of the system constantly shifting; in cases where it cannot organize the appropriate mass, it breaks into two parts. On the other hand, it can transform a weaker subject into its functionary without destroying it, and to a certain degree form a new unity with it. No 'substance', rather something that in itself strives after greater strength, and that wants to 'preserve' itself only indirectly (it wants to *surpass* itself).

(1968: 270)

PERSPECTIVISM

The revelation of will to power at the heart of life led Nietzsche to characterise being as a *process* rather than a substance. The world of substantial being is produced by the recombination of multiple effects of force into discrete ideas, images and identities. 'A thing is the sum of its effects', Nietzsche explains in *The Will To Power*, 'synthetically united by a concept, an image' (1968: 296). This is a crucial statement because it committed Nietzsche to a radical theory of truth based upon what he called *perspectivism* rather than positivism or the 'objective' reading of natural phenomena:

Against positivism, which halts at phenomena – 'There are only *facts*' – I would say: No, facts is precisely what there is not, only interpretations. We cannot establish any fact 'in itself': perhaps it is folly to want to do such a thing.

'Everything is subjective,' you say; but even this is interpretation. The 'subject' is not something given, it is something added and invented and projected behind what there is. – Finally, is it necessary to posit an interpreter behind the interpretation? Even this is invention, hypothesis.

In so far as the word 'knowledge' has any meaning, the world is knowable; but it is *interpretable* otherwise, it has no meaning behind it but countless meanings – 'Perspectivism.'

It is our needs that interpret the world; our drives and their For and Against. Every drive is a kind of lust to rule; each one has its perspective that it would like to compel all the other drives to accept as a norm.

(1968: 267)

This is a difficult passage requiring careful exegesis. Nietzsche's primary claim is that every natural 'fact' or 'truth' begins as an interpretation of life that wills a version of reality into existence. Mankind's habitual 'positivistic' error is to assume the existence of a commonly shared reality that functions as the objective standard for every interpretation of the world. Nietzsche objects to this assumption on two related grounds: there can be no 'general' theory of life or the world because this would imply a description *free* from perspective; and nothing – not even a theory of the world – can stand in the place of a general model of the 'real' because the properties of a 'thing' consist in its continuous *interrelationship* with other things. To understand the first objection, we must return to Nietzsche's belief that every general 'essence' – whether it be called 'life', 'being', 'substance', 'fact' or the 'world' – is produced by the historical dominance of a particular perspective that presupposes and delimits a multiplicity of other possible interpretations. Our vision of the world is therefore constituted by the interplay of perspectives brought to bear upon it; to make the world the criterion of truth for its interpretation is to transform an effect into a cause.

Will to power appears whenever an individual, group or institution reinterprets 'fact' to promote its own values and interests. Reinterpretation, we remember, always involves the assimilation of a weaker to a stronger force and this process necessarily creates a new perspective upon the world. We can illustrate this insight by attending to the successive reinterpretation of 'life' as a fact and a historical value. Thus for aristocratic culture 'life' was celebrated as a noble mode of self-expenditure and self-affirmation free from *ressentiment*. In contrast, the authority of priestly and ascetic culture was constituted by its reinterpretation of 'life' as an introspective mode of self-examination and denial in the service of a transcendent and spiritual life-to-come. Both aristocratic and priestly culture might speak in general terms of a 'good life' but the meaning of this description was produced by the perspective from which they chose to interpret the structure of human experience. Neither view has much in common with Nietzsche's own sardonic perspective upon existence: 'A multiplicity of forces, connected by a common mode of nutrition, we call "life"' (1968: 341). Nor should we expect these views to conform given Nietzsche's conviction that 'life' is produced as a meaning and value by the reinterpretation of experience – and the discontinuities that exist between old and new perspectives – rather than providing a general ground from which to judge the historical process.

Nietzsche's second objection radically extends this idea of meaning and value as effects of interpretation and will to power. He argues that the unity and coherence of a 'thing' is composed from the multiplicity of perspectives brought to bear upon it. The unity of an object is not guaranteed by a substance or identity subtending its various features; the object is brought into being by the will that interprets these features, links them one to another, and sets limits to the range of their association. Because interpretation always involves a struggle for domination between forces, a proper history of the formation of an object demands that we consider the principle of inclusion and exclusion that structures every form of life. Nietzsche's 'genealogical' mode of critique explicitly sets itself the task of understanding history as a movement of force and interpretation.

In a different spirit, the belief that a thing is the sum of its effects also motivates the American poet T. S. Eliot's view of literary 'tradition'. Eliot argues that that the relation between the 'traditional' and 'new' art work should not be understood as an orderly relation between two determinate entities: the meaning of both terms is produced simultaneously by the *perspective* that defines them within a common horizon. It is mistaken, Eliot continues, to assume that the 'existing monuments' of tradition possess intrinsic features independent of perspective that constitute a stable and timeless context for the interpretation of novelty (1951: 15). While it is true that tradition offers a context within which to read the new work of art, this context is simultaneously *transformed* by the introduction of novelty to the established order. The meaning of the new is, we might say, constituted and constituting: for order to persist after the supervention of novelty, Eliot concludes, 'the whole existing order must be, if ever so slightly, altered: and so the relations, proportions, values of each work of art toward the whole are readjusted; and this is conformity between the old and new' (1951: 15). The properties and resonances of traditional and new art are not, therefore, particular to their internal constitution or essence but defined instead by the 'conformity' or interpretative coherence conferred by the standards of historical communities of taste or reading practices in specific times and places. Eliot's modernist vision of a radicalised literary tradition thus reproduces the lesson of one of Nietzsche's most striking declarations: 'The properties of a thing are effects on other "things": if one removes other "things", then a thing has no properties, i.e. there is no thing without other "things", i.e. there is no "thing-in-itself"' (1968: 302).

The claim that there is no truth independent of interpretation is open to two types of objection. The first holds that to see 'truth' as a form of interpretation undermines the concept altogether. However, Nietzsche's point is not that 'there is no such thing as truth': to assert this as an axiomatic proposition would involve him in self-contradiction. He argues, instead, that there is no *one* perspective that is adequate to describe the world because the world may always be reinterpreted according to the values, interests and historical practices of different forms of life. And there are always perspectives on the world yet to come – one thinks of developments in microbiology, medicine and quantum physics – that might transform our preconceptions of the world into new beliefs and values. For an interpretation absolutely to describe the world it must be possible to conceive of the world independent of, and prior to, interpretation. But this is precisely what Nietzsche denies. Nor is it an adequate refutation of perspectivism to argue that because there may always be new interpretations of the world, every view is 'only' an interpretation and therefore of dubious legitimacy. To argue thus implies that there may be more certain views that are not interpretations. Yet as the influential Nietzsche scholar Alexander Nehamas has argued, it is not enough to declare that the view that all views are interpretations may be false; the challenge is to produce a view independent of interpretation:

> The view that all views are interpretations *may* be false; of what view does this not hold? To say that it might be false (which is all this claim amounts to) is not to say that it *is* false. . . . Perhaps not all views are interpretations. But we shall know this to be true only when one is actually produced.

> (1985: 67)

The second objection to perspectivism presents a modulation of the first. If it is true that everything is perspective and that it is through reinterpretation that will to power is expressed, have we not merely relapsed into a general and inflexible law of life that reproduces the dogmatic attitude Nietzsche strove to avoid? This objection presents Nietzsche with a genuine dilemma. However, this is not a problem of logical self-contradiction but rather the inevitable paradox produced whenever one is compelled to employ a metaphysical structure – the structure of language which divides reality into an opposition between subject and predicate and substance and property – to describe a process that *constitutes* every metaphysical concept. In this sense, Nietzsche could do no other than use language to describe a force of differentiation and reinterpretation that brings every structure of being into existence and determines their order and hierarchy. His only recourse was to insist that the structure of language could not exhaust the multiplicity of ways the world can be experienced. Thus while it remains true that we 'cease to think when we refuse to do so under the constraint of language' we must also acknowledge that the world so conceived 'seems logical to us because we have made it logical' (1968: 283). We should also be clear that Nietzsche's conviction that values represent dominant interpretations of life rather than absolute truth in no way commits him to a naive relativism. The fact that other perspectives upon the world are always possible does *not* make each perspective equally valuable. A perspective is a reinterpretation of existence, and Nietzsche is unequivocal that the most powerful perspectives transform reactive into active forms of life. The value of a perspective is the quantity of will to power that it expresses and the affirmative power of the life it makes possible. Another interpretation of life is always possible – an aristocratic culture may be replaced by the slave revolt in morals – but this should be seen as the redirection of will to power to narrow and reactive ends.

POWER, TRAGEDY AND AFFIRMATION

To consider existence from the viewpoint of perspectivism is to discover will to power at the heart of every concept, image and condition of life. This view enables us to abjure the vulgar impression of will to power as merely a psychological expression of violent domination; it appears instead as a vision of the emergence of states of being and forms of truth. The coupling of 'being' and 'truth' is not arbitrary: Nietzsche consistently links will to power to what he calls the 'will to truth' in order to underline his contention that 'truth' describes the reinterpretation and creative ordering of the world rather than the discovery of a series of 'natural' facts. 'Truth', Nietzsche reminds us in *The Will To Power*, is 'not something there, that might be found or discovered – but something that must be created and that gives a name to a process, or rather to a will to overcome that has in itself no end' (1968: 298). Truth, in fact, is 'a word for the will to power'. The more powerful a force of life becomes, the greater its capacity to impose the 'truth' of its vision of existence upon the world (p. 299). What Nietzsche calls a 'value' does not correspond to an objective or absolute truth: it represents the 'highest quantum of power' that a being can incorporate before it is transformed into something else (p. 380). Values, in this sense, always have a reactive dimension because they are ways of preserving a condition of life. The metaphysical belief in truth is fundamental to the consolidation of values because 'truth' consists in the transformation of *quantities* of force into moral and ethical *qualities*. The simplest way for a conditional value to become authoritative, after all, is for it to repress the history of its emergence and present itself as a 'quality' of 'man' and a timeless truth.

If every value is produced by a struggle for mastery between different perspectives, it follows that will to power must form the basis for *both* active and reactive interpretations of the world. It is clear that the spontaneous and active self-assertion of aristocratic being expresses a pre-reflective will to power that was challenged and ultimately reinterpreted by the 'bad conscience' of Christianity and slave morality. But, as we have seen, Nietzsche also characterises the reactive development of the ascetic ideal as a will to power that 'springs from the protective and healing instincts of a degenerating life which uses every means to maintain itself and struggles for its existence' (2000: 93). Nietzsche's castigation of pity stemmed from the negative aspect of the will to power that it expresses: to pity oneself is to preserve the weak features of one's character that should rather be overcome; while pity for others always involves a degree of condescension and a consciousness of one's own superior power. We might say that the negative aspect of will to power originates in a freedom *from* a particular configuration of forces (other people, the state, aristocratic culture and so on), while the positive experience of power is experienced in the power *to* overcome these forces and assimilate them to ourselves. Both reactive and active being, then, express a will to power: the transition from the former to the latter takes place when a being overcomes itself and achieves predominance within an unequal distribution of forces rather than existing as the effect of a descending form of life. For this reason it is mistaken simply to present autonomous individualism as the highest manifestation of will to power; individualism is, Nietzsche cautions, only 'the *most modest* stage of the will to power' (1968: 412). Freedom and self-determination are merely the preliminary stages of a movement of self-overcoming that produces hierarchies of power and the emergence of a *higher type*:

My ideas do not revolve around the degree of freedom that is granted to the one or to the other or to all, but around the degree of *power* that the one or the other should exercise over others or over all, and to what extent a sacrifice of freedom, even enslavement, provides the basis for the emergence of a *higher type*.

(1968: 458)

A philosophy that seeks to cultivate self-overcoming and the strongest forces of life culminates, Nietzsche concluded, in the apotheosis of *art*. The artist is the ultimate exponent of will to power for Nietzsche because 'art' expresses the power to create a vision of the world from one's own perspective in order to maximise one's own force and authority. Art therefore has the potential to overcome *ressentiment*: the weak and reactive vision of life that judges every force stronger than our own as evil and repressive. To embrace the will to power, on the other hand, means to affirm the entire network of forces that creates positions and laws, rather than adopting a fixed and inflexible position that tries to hamper the emergence of new forces. This contrast between *ressentiment* and will to power lies at the core of Virginia Woolf's (1882–1941) novel *To the Lighthouse* (1927). Woolf's novel appears, at first glance, to reveal the success of *ressentiment* in constructing an orderly and coherent vision of the world. This vision is underpinned by the dichotomy *To the Lighthouse* appears to present between masculine reason and feminine imagination and intuitiveness. These positions are represented by the philosopher Mr Ramsey and his acolyte Charles Tansley on one hand, and on the other by the impressionist painter Lily Briscoe. Philosophy, in this context, connotes a masculine ideal of logic, reason and truth that is assumed to transcend a narrowly 'feminine' world of domestic care, emotional sensibility and intellectual vagueness, one that is inhabited by the philosopher's self-effacing wife Mrs Ramsey. The elevation of the masculine sphere of thought and accomplishment over the feminine world of feeling and intuition is underscored by Tansley's dismissive refrain 'women can't write, women can't paint', which situates the feminine altogether beyond the limit of truth and rational representation (Woolf 1984: 81). Here, in Tansley's sterile and reactive vision of life, we can see the principle of *ressentiment* in action. Women, for him, cannot affirm life because they cannot give it coherence and logical order. They therefore *deny* life, and must be spoken for by the (masculine) intelligence capable of discerning a rational order within our experience. An image of feminine experience as formless, chaotic and valueless is thus created; and this degraded image reciprocally privileges the qualities of order and rationality ascribed to masculine thought.

To the Lighthouse elaborates this principle of *ressentiment* while expressing another vision of life that exceeds its narrow boundaries. This other vision is explicitly associated with Lily Briscoe's art. Briscoe's painting is sneered at by Tansley, who is unsettled by an aesthetic that bears no relation to his own way of seeing the world. For what distinguishes Briscoe's artistic vision is its refusal to conform to either the masculine model of the truth of life as logic, reason and representation or its feminine reinterpretation as subjectivity, intuition and bodily affect. Instead, her art records an impersonal and spontaneous act of creation that plunges us back into the chaos and force of life. Her work does not express a self or seek to represent a non-self. It affirms a world of multiple becoming, or force without form, that creates every truth and value. Lines of light and the energy of becoming: this is the 'other' reality that presses upon her as her art moves beyond form and representation:

> With a curious physical sensation, as if she were urged forward and at the same time must hold herself back, she made her first quick decisive stroke. The brush descended. It flickered brown over the white canvas; it left a running mark. A second time she did it – a third time. And so pausing and so flickering, she attained a dancing rhythmical movement, as if the pauses were one part of the rhythm and the strokes another, and all were related; and so, lightly and swiftly pausing, she scored her canvas with brown running nervous lines which had no sooner settled there than they enclosed (she felt it looming out at her) a space. Down in the hollow of one wave she saw the next wave towering higher and higher above her. For what could be more formidable than that space? Here she was again, she thought, stepping back to look at it, drawn out of gossip, out of living, out of community with people into the presence of this formidable ancient enemy of hers – this other thing, this truth, this reality, which suddenly laid hands on her, emerged stark at the back of appearances and commanded her attention.

> (Woolf 1984: 148)

Art, in this Nietzschean sense, is constitutive of every truth about the world we possess. It is the wilful invention or self-consciously asserted perspective that brings truth into being; its power inheres in the creation of concepts like 'identity' and 'difference', 'being' and 'becoming', and 'truth' and 'appearance' that structure the metaphysical interpretation of reality. 'Before there is "thought",' Nietzsche declares, 'there must have been "invention"; the *construction* of identical cases, of the appearance of sameness, is more primitive than the knowledge of sameness' (1968: 293). However, the paradox and power of art for Nietzsche is that while it supplies the creative perspective that orders conceptual thought, it also provides an experience of force and becoming that *transcends* truth and morality. The force of art cannot be exhausted by the concepts it creates; art is 'more divine' than morality and 'worth more' than truth because it demonstrates that every truth is an interpretation and that no one interpretation can ever adequately account for the world (p. 453). To perceive the world as the artful construction of will to power means to recognise an immanent and univocal force at the heart of life. From this perspective, the division between 'reality' and 'appearance' that underpinned Nietzsche's early work is itself the effect of a reactive mode of thought. To posit a world of appearance is to presuppose a more authentic world that *appears*. For Nietzsche, the very secondariness of the concept of appearance – the idea that a distinct world appears to us and is *then* valued – belies the force that produces perspectives.

> The apparent world, i.e., a world viewed according to values; ordered, selected according to values, i.e., in this case according to the viewpoint of utility in regard to the preservation and enhancement of the power of a certain species of animal.
>
> The perspective therefore decides the character of the 'appearance'! As if a world would still remain over after one deducted the perspective! By doing that one would deduct relativity!
>
> Every center of force adopts a perspective towards the entire remainder, i.e., its own particular valuation, mode of action, and mode of resistance. The 'apparent world', therefore, is reduced to a specific mode of action on the world, emanating from a center.
>
> Now there is no other mode of action whatever; and the 'world' is only a word for the totality of these actions. Reality consists precisely in this particular action and reaction of every individual part toward the whole –
>
> No shadow of a right remains to speak here of *appearance* –
>
> (1968: 305)

In order to achieve the strength to experience the world as will to power, Nietzsche argues, we must develop a *tragic* perspective upon life. 'Tragedy', we recall from his early work, should not be understood here in the classical sense as submission to a malign destiny; to live tragically, as Nietzsche's mature thought makes clear, is to have the strength to impose an interpretation upon the total economy of forces that constitute every form of life. Tragic existence is a mode of *positivity* because it seeks to create truths and values beyond the reactive division between good and evil. It also provides the most profound possible experience of *affirmation* insofar as it accepts the interconnectedness of every level of life and produces an 'absolute affirmation of the world' (1968: 527). This tragic vision of life as a process of dynamic inter-relation acknowledges 'error', illusion and force as the pre-condition of 'truth' and identifies cruelty, violence and suffering at the origin of morality. The 'profundity' of tragic being lies for Nietzsche in its affirmation of 'the *large-scale economy* which justifies *the terrifying, the evil, the questionable*' without recourse to an established moral system (p. 451). Weak natures renounce active force by denying their own will to power and discovering ultimate value in the 'triumph of the moral world-order' (p. 450). The powerful and tragic nature, in contrast, produces values by the differentiation of active from reactive force and the creation of a pathos of distance. Tragedy as a process of creative self-constitution is therefore an experience of 'Dionysian joy' and an overcoming of every nihilistic sentiment (p. 531).

In a note written in the last sane year of his life, Nietzsche brought together will to power and tragic affirmation and made them the funda-mental challenge of his philosophy: 'How much truth can a spirit *endure*, how much truth does a spirit *dare*? – this became for me the real stan-dard of value' (1968: 536). Those who would answer such a question must be prepared to embrace nihilism – the devaluation of all estab-lished values – in order to pass beyond nihilism towards 'a Dionysian affirmation of the world as it is, without subtraction, exception or selection' and the 'eternal circulation'. Nietzsche's famous description of his thought as 'philosophising with a hammer' means precisely this: to develop an 'ecstatic nihilism' that might *overcome* nihilism and reverse the 'moralisation' of 'man' as a creature of sin and bad conscience (p. 544). He insistently linked together will to power, eternal recur-rence and *amor fati* because each is an immanent principle of force and becoming that is opposed to a transcendent spirit beyond life that judges life. 'This world is the will to power', Nietzsche proclaimed, 'and nothing besides!' (p. 550). The development of a philosophy of will to power accounts for his enigmatic statement at the end of *Ecce Homo*: 'Have I been understood? *Dionysos against the Crucified*' (1992: 104). The more Nietzsche reflected upon will to power as a tragic philosophy of life and a return to the Greek 'pessimism of strength', the more he realised that Christ, not Apollo, was the real antithesis to a Dionysiac state conceived as 'an ecstatic affirmation of the total character of life' (1968: 539). Here, in his last writings, Nietzsche described the fullest measure of will to power as the affirmation of a tragic value to suffering and the overcoming of *ressentiment* and the reactive interpretation of life:

Dionysius versus the 'Crucified': there you have the antithesis. It is *not* a difference in regard to their martyrdom – it is a difference in the meaning of it. Life itself, its eternal fruitfulness and recurrence, creates torment, destruction, the will to annihilation. In the other case, suffering – the 'Crucified as the innocent one' – counts as an objection to this life, as a formula for its condemnation. One will see that the problem is that of the meaning of suffering: whether a Christian meaning or a tragic meaning. In the former case, it is supposed to be the path to a holy existence; in the latter case, being is counted as *holy enough* to justify even a monstrous amount of suffering. The tragic man affirms even the harshest suffering: he is sufficiently strong, rich, and capable of deifying to do so. The Christian denies even the happiest lot on earth: he is sufficiently weak, poor, disinherited to suffer from life in whatever form he meets it. The god on the cross is a curse on life, a signpost to seek redemption from life; Dionysius cut to pieces is a *promise* of life: it will be eternally reborn and return again from destruction.

(1968: 542–543)

SUMMARY

Nietzsche's conception of the will to power describes a principle of life that is interior to life rather than a metaphysical concept above and beyond life such as transcendental reason. It presents all life, not just human life, as united by a common striving for power. Will to power liberates us from representing existence merely in anthropomorphic terms by announcing an inhuman principle of creation that both constitutes and exceeds human life. All life is a continuum created by an inhuman will to power that produces human consciousness and identity as one of its effects. The aim of life is neither self-preservation nor moral and spiritual enlightenment but the increase of power and the pursuit of dominion. The will to power interprets existence by identifying a hierarchy of forces between different forms of life and judging how far one force has become master of another. The hierarchy of force represented by the dominance of a particular perspective upon life over other perspectives is the basis for the formation of every 'truth' and 'value'. There is no 'real' world behind this hierarchical play of perspectives; will to power is the productive force that constitutes every level of life. Consequently, the conflict between interpretations and the quest for dominion becomes fundamental to our experience of being.

AFTER NIETZSCHE

Despite Nietzsche's relative critical neglect during his lifetime, his ideas have enjoyed a spectacular renaissance over the last hundred years. This influence has been particularly marked since the Second World War, when the French rediscovery of his work led to an enormous burgeoning of Nietzsche studies. Nietzsche's legacy has been both profound and controversial, which is unsurprising granted the provocative force of his statements about politics, morality, art and culture. The dubious alignment of his name with the politics of Nazism has haunted Nietzsche studies for half a century, and his political writing remains a subject of fierce debate. At the same time, his ideas have had an enormously energising effect upon areas as diverse as aesthetics, literature, ethics, political and social theory, history and psychology. This influence is now so pervasive that it seems inadequate to engage in discussion about what it means to be human without invoking Nietzsche's name. In this concluding chapter, we will examine the ways in which Nietzsche's work has influenced some of these areas, looking briefly at the effect his ideas have had upon a range of artists and thinkers.

NIETZSCHE'S INFLUENCE

The first two important books designed to introduce Nietzsche's work to the general public were Lou Salome's *Friedrich Nietzsche: The Man in*

His Work (1894) and Elizabeth Förster-Nietzsche's two-volume *The Life of Friedrich Nietzsche* (1895 and 1897). Lou Salome (1861–1937) was an intellectual, poet and freethinker who captivated Nietzsche and to whom he proposed marriage unsuccessfully in 1882. Her book highlighted two themes: the fundamental importance of the *style* of Nietzsche's work (with its use of aphorism, multiple voices and different types of narrative perspective), and also the relationship between physical and mental vitality or decline to the production of his ideas. These ideas have become staples of Nietzsche criticism, although Salome's considerable emphasis upon the second point did much to create an image of him in the public mind as a neurotic and decadent genius. Certainly this representation of Nietzsche as a transgressive, excessive and decadent writer was fiercely contested by Elizabeth Förster-Nietzsche, always jealous of Salome's hold over her brother. Elizabeth's book offered a contrasting image of Nietzsche as a healthy, outgoing, manifestly sane and adventurous thinker gradually developing the tenets of a coherent and systematic philosophy. Elizabeth's real significance, however, lies in the control she exercised over Nietzsche's work after his breakdown in 1889. She assumed the legal rights to her brother's complete literary estate in 1895 and used this authority to re-order his unpublished notes into a new 'work' entitled *The Will to Power* (published first in German in 1901, and reissued in a massively expanded edition in 1906). *The Will to Power* has exerted a powerful influence upon Nietzsche's reputation ever since, and the title's selective focus upon 'will' and 'power' did much to reinforce his image in the first half of the last century as a champion of physical force and violence. The book's influence is particularly problematic for two reasons: Nietzsche never saw this 'book' into print – indeed, it contains a quantity of notes he explicitly discarded – and therefore its authenticity remains a matter of great scholarly dispute; and the selection of notes it contains appears to reflect a consistently unifying philosophical principle to his work in the principles of will to power and the eternal recurrence, whereas his other books employ them within the broader context of his revaluation of all values.

The cumulative effect of these early readings of Nietzsche and the publication of *The Will to Power* was to produce an image of Nietzsche as both an 'extreme' and 'literary' philosopher whose work represented a revolutionary challenge to late nineteenth-century bourgeois and Christian culture. The overt romanticism of this image perhaps explains why Nietzsche's writing found its first receptive audience within the artistic, rather than the philosophical, community. Certainly his work had an immense impact upon the movement known as 'literary modernism'. To cite only the most famous examples, Nietzsche's reflections upon culture, art and value resonate throughout the work of W. B Yeats (1865–1939), D. H. Lawrence (1885–1930) and Thomas Mann (1875–1955), while the concept of the *Übermensch* or 'superman' is ironically reworked in George Bernard Shaw's play *Man and Superman* of 1903.

The first major philosophical consideration of Nietzsche's work was published in 1935 by the German philosopher Karl Jaspers (1883–1969) under the title *Nietzsche: An Introduction to the Understanding of his Philosophical Activity*. Jaspers' book, which focused in particular upon Nietzsche's reinterpretation of morality and the meaning of 'man', was followed by Martin Heidegger's (1889–1976) four-volume *Nietzsche* (a collection of Heidegger's lecture notes, published in 1961). Heidegger's reading of Nietzsche is also an attack on the western philosophical tradition in general. Heidegger, who relied heavily on *The Will to Power*, claimed that Nietzsche's insistence on life as force and will was anything but a radical anti-metaphysical manoeuvre. In his attempt to explain all concepts through one principle of life as power, Nietzsche merely repeated the metaphysical tendency to reduce being to the ideas we have of it. Instead of Nietzsche's one life or *bios*, Heidegger insisted that we need to rethink how we come to *know* or *disclose* life. Heidegger, like Nietzsche, was also associated with Nazism, precisely because he thought that only National Socialism could liberate German thought from the reduction to mere life of which Nietzsche was guilty.

The power and provocation of Heidegger's reading of Nietzsche was felt particularly in post-war France, where it helped to inspire a number of major reinterpretations of the Nietzschean inheritance that came to be known as 'the New Nietzsche'. Against the Heideggerean reading of Nietzsche as a metaphysician, the French Nietzscheans focused more upon the literary and stylistic aspects of Nietzsche's work that disrupted conceptual thinking. A number of important readings of Nietzsche have appeared in France since the early 1960s, among the most notable of which are Gilles Deleuze's *Nietzsche and Philosophy* of 1962, Michel Foucault's essay 'Nietzsche, Genealogy, History' of 1971, Jacques Derrida's *Spurs*, of 1978, and Sarah Kofman's *Nietzsche and Metaphor*, of 1978. These works are not only significant in their own right, they also reveal Nietzsche's influence upon contemporary readings of history, theories of power and the radical hermeneutics characteristic of the 'deconstructive turn' in philosophy.

ART

Nietzsche's work, as noted earlier, has had a pervasive influence upon modern literature. This influence is particularly evident in the work of Thomas Mann, D. H. Lawrence and W. B Yeats. Mann's novella *Death in Venice* (1912) examines the role of the artist within modern culture by reworking the Nietzschean relationship between Apollo and Dionysius. Its protagonist, the writer Gustav Von Aschenbach, has become one of the most celebrated chroniclers of the modern German spirit. However, Aschenbach's art is eventually made sterile by its elevation of Apollonian form, order and morality over the Dionysiac elements of myth, sexuality and passion. In the story of Aschenbach's rejection of his secure position within bourgeois society, his journey to Venice and his fatal erotic infatuation with the beautiful Polish boy Tadzio, Mann follows Nietzsche in suggesting that modern art and culture needs to discover a productive relationship between the primal and mythic forces of life and the aesthetic structures that enable us to experience these forces without being destroyed by them.

D. H. Lawrence's novella *The Ladybird* (1923) also draws heavily upon the dialectical relationship between Apollo and Dionysius. It describes the relationship between an aristocratic English woman, Lady Daphne Beveridge, and the Bohemian Count Johann Dionys Psanek, who is confined as a prisoner of war in London. Before meeting Count Dionys, Daphne is weary and sick at heart; her life is defined by a hollow commitment to social convention and an exhausted Christian moralism. She represents the decadence of Apollonian ideals when they become divorced from Dionysiac passion and vitality: 'the curious, distraught slant of her eyes told of a wild energy damned up inside her' (Lawrence 1985: 13). This energy is released by the Dionysiac force of Count Dionys, who embodies a dark, sensual and primal vitality that shakes Daphne's world to its foundations. Dionys dreams of a 'god of destruction' who will sweep away what he sees as the sterile egalitarianism of modern bourgeois existence and confer power upon the aristocratic type able 'to choose and to command' (1985: 42, 59). In Lawrence's Nietzschean fable, the separation of Apollonian form and Dionysiac energy subordinates life to outmoded social norms and values; it is only when public morality once more encounters the transfiguring power of Dionysis that it becomes possible to conceive new possibilities of living.

Nietzschean echoes may also be detected in W. B. Yeats's apocalyptic poem 'The Second Coming' (1921), in which the 'centre' of an entire western Christian tradition 'cannot hold' and 'mere anarchy is loosed upon the world'. 'The Second Coming' offers a terrifying depiction of the nihilism of modern western culture: the devaluation of traditional moral and spiritual values with nothing available to take their place. This nihilistic theme is reinforced by Yeats's image of the 'widening gyre' of history in the poem's opening line. For Yeats history was constituted by fundamentally opposed forces: as western culture lurches towards the second millennium since the birth of Christ, another cycle of history is about to begin in which Christian values will be meaningless. This coming era precipitates the dissolution of modern culture where 'The best lack all conviction, while the worst | are full of passionate intensity' (1975: 100). 'The Second Coming' concludes with the specifically anti-Christian image of a 'rough beast', half-human and half-animal, slouching towards Bethlehem to be born. Violence is prefigured everywhere in the poem because a metamorphosis in our moral and spiritual values is taking place without the order and coherence that might be imposed by a strong and creative spirit. What modern history requires, Yeats implies in his most Nietzschean vein, is a new visionary intensity in order to create new forms and values capable of transforming the conditions of contemporary life. There are more subtle Nietzschean references in Yeats's other poems, including 'Among School Children', where the question 'How can we tell the dancer from the dance?' echoes Nietzsche's refusal to separate a 'doer' from the 'deed'.

RETHINKING HISTORY

Nietzsche's influence is also clearly evident in the critical practice of 'new historicism', which has gained prominence in literary studies and cultural theory. The work of new historicist writers such as Stephen Greenblatt, Louis Montrose and Christine Gallacher presents a 'new' way of reading the relationship between particular texts – Renaissance drama, travel writing, medical documents and so on – and their historical context that is heavily indebted to Nietzsche's genealogical critique, particularly in the forms in which it was represented in the work of the French philosopher Michel Foucault (1926–84). Like Nietzsche, new historicist writers challenge the idea that history constitutes a stable and continuous general context against which the meanings of texts and events may be established. While historicist thinkers might interpret historical events by situating them within the 'world view' or 'ideology' of a particular period or social system, 'new' historicism attends to local and particular historical phenomena before it is assimilated into general discursive constructs like 'sixteenth-century history' or 'Renaissance culture'. An analysis of Renaissance culture undertaken by Greenblatt (1992) typically proceeds by rehearsing seemingly peripheral anecdotes and oral testimony rather than extracts from established public documents. It examines the history of Renaissance England in terms of the discontinuous and often antagonistic relationship between different forms of historical inscription: court protocol, church liturgy, myth and folklore, jurisprudence, the contextual spaces of architecture and theatrical performance and so on – in order to focus upon the way that the boundaries between historical texts and contexts are produced and legitimated. New historicism's emphasis upon the multiple, ad hoc and contingent character of historical narratives offers a corrective to monolithic conceptions of ideology and historical periodicity, and high- lights the constitutive role of the present in determining the meaning of the past. New historicist writers also draw upon Nietzsche's work for their assertion that the construction of the self is an effect of power. Identity is not seen in their work as the reflection of an innate and meta- physical essence; it is fashioned and produced by external and contingent effects like codes of dress, forms of rhetoric and the theatrical perform- ance of gesture and ritual.

PHILOSOPHY AFTER NIETZSCHE

A third area in which Nietzsche's work has proved influential is conti- nental European philosophy. This influence is particularly marked in the philosophical movement known as 'existentialism', which is most closely associated with the work of the French philosopher Jean-Paul Sartre (1905–80). One of the primary tenets of existentialism is that 'existence precedes essence'. Men and women are born into a godless world without divine guidance or the promise of redemption. Because human life is necessarily lived in the absence of transcendental values or moral structures, the ethical purpose of existence for Sartre is for humanity actively to create its values for itself and to develop a style of living and thinking that continually redefines the meaning of what it is to be human. Nietzsche's influence also appears in the work of the Algerian philosopher Jacques Derrida. Derrida's work, which is now largely synonymous with the terms 'post-structuralism' and 'deconstruction', follows Nietzsche in considering philosophical concepts as the *effect* of movements of force and difference. In works such as the essays collected in *Writing and Difference* (1978), Derrida challenged the 'structuralist' mode of analysis pioneered by the linguist Ferdinand de Saussure (1857–1913), which sought to move beyond a theory of meaning and knowledge centred upon 'man' or the intentional self-awareness of the human subject by attending instead to the structures – language, signs and concepts – that make human discourse meaningful in the first place. Derrida's response follows Nietzsche in placing emphasis upon the differential forces – the movement of spacing and temporal delay Derrida christens 'differance' – that simultaneously constitute and exceed every 'closed' structure. Derrida's focus upon the way in which the metaphorical play of language always opens texts up to doubled or supplementary readings also recalls Nietzsche's work on metaphor and conceptuality and has proved massively influential in literary and cultural studies. This deconstructive approach to language and conceptuality became the intellectual inspiration for the 'Yale School' of literary critics. One of the most prominent members of this group, Paul de Man (1919–83), devoted three essays of his *Allegories of Reading: Figural Language in Rousseau, Nietzsche, Rilke and Proust* (1979) to a deconstructive reading of *The Birth of Tragedy*.

Nietzsche's legacy also proved crucial to the work of the French philosopher Gilles Deleuze (1925–95). For Deleuze, like Nietzsche, the fundamental activity of philosophy was the creation of concepts. The problem with thought, Deleuze argued, lies in its desire for *transcendence*: the ascription of an ideal outside life (such as 'God' or the 'moral' individual) that determines the goal and value of life. Conversely, Deleuze sought to move beyond our commitment to transcendence and engage with the broader movements of becoming from which our idea of life is constituted. He therefore focused upon the different forms of difference – such as language, historical events, social forms, genetic developments and mutations and so on – that precede thought and bring it into being. Following Nietzsche, Deleuze develops the concept of *affect* (our investment in feeling, emotion and desire) to rethink the meaning and function of contemporary politics. Contemporary politics, Deleuze argues, is determined by the notion of ideology and the conception of the 'political' as a meaningful exchange between self-conscious and rational agents. On this model, 'ideology' and 'politics' are structures that impose themselves upon and negatively delimit the identity of the social and political individual. Thus one is a 'good' worker if one invests in the productive dynamic of market capitalism, a 'feminine' woman if one adheres to various protocols of dress, image, taste and language, and morally 'respectable' if one genuflects to the pieties of Christian rhetoric. However, Deleuze challenges the assumption of the ideological determination of social codes by emphasising instead the production of our notions of politics, ideology and subjectivity by a series of 'inhuman' or pre-subjective styles and intensities. Before there is a rational or political decision, Deleuze claims, there is an unconscious and positive affective investment in *images and styles* of morality. We invest in an image and style of morality that is then reconfigured as the moral ground of life itself. Thus an investment in the authority of the father is also, for Deleuze, an investment in the banker, the cop, the soldier and the businessman (Deleuze and Guattari 1984: 97). What we call 'ideology' and 'politics' is constituted from these affective investments, which are then relayed back to us as the universal ground of order and control.

FEMINISM

It may appear surprising to suggest that Nietzsche's work has also had a signal effect upon feminism, given his many dismissive references to woman and the infamous line from *Thus Spoke Zarathustra*, 'Are you visiting women? Do not forget your whip' (1969: 93). However, key elements of the Nietzschean revaluation of values have had a lasting influence upon the feminist critique of patriarchal power. Nietzsche's emphasis upon the historical constitution of values and his perception of subjectivity as an embodied effect of will to power supply a useful context for feminist thinkers working to expose patriarchy as a political and cultural construction rather than a neutral description of a biological hierarchy (Gross, in Patton 1993: 54). The new style of writing that Nietzsche developed in order to subvert the metaphysical grammar of reason has also influenced feminists seeking to resist the patriarchal identification of reason and logic with masculinity. By following Nietzsche in showing that every cultural and philosophical discourse represents the will to power of a particular perspective upon life, these writers have demonstrated that the association of the feminine with corporeality, irrationality and sensuality is a historical interpretation of being that lies open to challenge and revision (Irigaray 1991; Kofman 1993). Nietzsche's theory of *ressentiment* has also been invoked by feminists to provide a critical focus upon the mutation of aspects of feminist practice into negative and resentful forms of will to power. Thus the contemporary Australian philosopher Marion Tapper argues that too much recent feminist theory and practice has moved away from an analysis of specific issues of injustice and discrimination and broadened into a general and pejorative critique of masculinity and 'western reason'. Tapper characterises this type of practice as classic *ressentiment*: it is backward-looking and expansive (always looking for new injustices); obsessed with detecting 'evil' in the very nature of language, culture and society; and concerned only with a reactive vision of power seen as the power to dominate (Tapper, in Patton 1993: 134).

Nietzsche's influence upon contemporary thought is growing all the time, particularly since the work of French post-structuralists began to be translated in the 1970s and 1980s. This new receptivity to Nietzsche's work culminated in the publication of an influential collection of essays exploring Nietzsche's legacy entitled *The New Nietzsche* in 1985. Apart from a general influence upon post-structuralism, which stresses that there can be no *single* structure that explains or organises experience, there has been both affirmation and criticism of Nietzsche's thought by key post-structuralist thinkers. On the one hand, writers such as Jacques Derrida, Michel Foucault, Gilles Deleuze and Luce Irigaray have sustained and intensified Nietzsche's attack on 'man'. On the other hand, these writers have also perceived a need to go beyond Nietzsche. Derrida's *Spurs* (1979), Foucault's *The Order of Things* (1992), Irigaray's *Marine Lover* (1991) and Deleuze's *Difference and Repetition* (1994) have all insisted that Nietzsche's 'influence' extends well beyond the explicit themes of his work and prompts radical questions about *how* to think. Because Nietzsche's thought reflects upon central questions of power and responsibility, the nature of subjectivity, the purpose and value of morality, the proper direction of modernity and the meaning of the 'human' when the relation between self and world is continually in process, this influence looks set to last for a long time to come.

FURTHER READING

WORKS BY FRIEDRICH NIETZSCHE

All the texts discussed in this book are available in English translation. Many students first encounter Nietzsche's work through his 'scandalous' books, *Beyond Good and Evil*, *On the Genealogy of Morality* and *Twilight of the Idols*. These books are perhaps the best place to start because they convey the shock and provocation of Nietzsche's work while drawing attention to some of his major themes. They are complex and challenging, like all of Nietzsche's philosophy, but also contain many polemical passages that give the reader a sense of why he argued for an 'immoral' and 'aristocratic' style of thought. Once you have had time to come to terms with some of Nietzsche's most powerful and influential ideas, it makes sense to return to his early work. You would then be in a position to gain a concrete impression of what Nietzsche thought he was reacting against and why he thought his intellectual revolt was necessary and valuable. Certainly *The Birth of Tragedy*, which can seem a strange and puzzling text, benefits enormously from being read in the context of his later work. The development of Nietzsche's ideas from *Untimely Meditations* to *Human, All Too Human*, *Daybreak* and *The Gay Science* (with its enigmatic reflections on eternal recurrence and the 'Death of God') also becomes easier to understand once you have already been exposed to Nietzsche's aphoristic style. By this stage, you should be ready to come to grips with *Thus Spoke Zarathustra*. *Zarathustra* is not necessarily more difficult than Nietzsche's other works, but its poetic use of fable is apt to appear off-putting unless you have a secure sense of Nietzsche's principal ideas. Nietzsche's autobiography, *Ecce Homo*, is instructive, amusing and disturbing in turn, but should be read for the occasional light it sheds upon his major concepts rather than as an authoritative and final authorial judgement on his entire corpus; Nietzsche wrote *Ecce Homo* on the edge of mental collapse, and the text shows signs of his deterioration in its pages. *The Will to Power* must also be treated with a degree of caution, because it contains Nietzsche's unpublished – and sometimes discarded – notes. Its inevitable lack of narrative coherence probably makes it suitable only for the reader who has read and digested most of Nietzsche's published work and wants to discover more about his working method.

In this section, Nietzsche's works are ordered either by their original publication date, or, for those books which were unpublished in his lifetime, by the date at which they were written. In this way, you should be able to get a clear idea of both his writing and publishing career. All the works listed originally appeared in German. The publication details here indicate the English versions that you will most likely consult. For this reason, two dates appear in most of the entries. For books published in Nietzsche's lifetime, the first date in square brackets is the original publication date, while the second date and all the other details refer to the translation. However, for books unpublished in Nietzsche's lifetime, only the date of the edition you are most likely to consult is given, while some reference to the date at which the book was written is incorporated into the brief description of its contents.

[1872] (1993) *The Birth of Tragedy*, trans. Shaun Whiteside, Harmondsworth: Penguin.

This was Nietzsche's first book. It presents his theory of the birth and demise of Greek tragedy, the beginnings of his critique of moral thought and his reflection upon the possibility of a non-moral approach to life.

[1873] (1999) 'On Truth and Lying in a Non-Moral Sense', in *The Birth of Tragedy and Other Writings*, trans. Ronald Spiers, Cambridge: Cambridge University Press.

This short early essay, unpublished in Nietzsche's lifetime, presents one of his most provocative and influential analyses of the history and function of truth. Nietzsche argues that as human culture and society developed, humanity gradually forgot that truth originated as a metaphor that allowed us to impose our peculiarly anthropomorphic values and perspectives upon life. Although this essay is frequently quoted, it has often proved inaccessible in print. This edition offers the most readily available version of the complete text.

[1873–5] (1997c) *Untimely Meditations*, trans. R. J. Hollingdale, Cambridge: Cambridge University Press.

These four essays present Nietzsche's early critique of modern German culture, morality and the historical sense, and explore his relationship to the philosopher Arthur Schopenhauer and the composer Richard Wagner. These works are now widely neglected, but they remain indispensable to an understanding of Nietzsche's views upon history, tradition, art and culture. The second essay, 'On the Uses and Disadvantages of History for Life', also provides one of Nietzsche's earliest and most leisurely reflections upon the difference between historical consciousness and what he came to define as his own genealogical mode of thought.

[Unpublished in Nietzsche's lifetime] (1997b) *Philosophy and Truth: Selections from Nietzsche's Notebooks of the Early 1870s*, ed. and trans. Daniel Breazeale, Atlantic Highlands, NJ: Humanities Press.

An important collection of six previously unpublished early manuscripts written between 1872 and 1876 just after *The Birth of Tragedy* and simultaneously with *Untimely Meditations*, which explore Nietzsche's views on philosophy, culture, and the Greeks.

[1879] (1984) *Human, All Too Human*, trans. Marion Feber and Stephen Lehmann, Harmondsworth: Penguin.

A crucial collection of aphorisms in which Nietzsche broke with the metaphysical assumptions of his early work, and began to develop some of his most distinctive themes, such as the will to power, the idea of aristocratic culture and slavish nature, and his critique of truth. This text was also the first in which he made the transition to an aphoristic style of writing. Now we encounter the idiosyncratic and playful form of Nietzsche's mature work, in which the reader is constantly confronted with perspectives and points of view that challenge his most cherished assumptions. Often disturbing and always provocative, the text functions as a microcosm of Nietzsche's thought as a whole.

[1881] (1997a) *Daybreak: Thoughts on the Prejudices of Morality*, trans. R. J. Hollingdale, Cambridge: Cambridge University Press.

A wide-ranging and sustained critique of the presuppositions and prejudices of both morality and modern philosophy from Kant to Schopenhauer, and a decisive step towards Nietzsche's revaluation of all values.

[1882] (1974) *The Gay Science: With a Prelude in Rhymes and an Appendix of Songs*, trans. Walter Kaufmann, New York: Vintage.

The reputation of *The Gay Science* as one of Nietzsche's most significant works continues to grow. Its five books contain nearly four hundred aphorisms, which offer a fascinating overview of his assault on the moral interpretation of existence and his revaluation of all values. This text is wide-ranging and challenging, but also funny, engaging and often colloquial in tone. It is also extremely clear in signalling the scope and ambition of Nietzsche's intellectual project because it returns to his philosophical roots in the Greek exploration of what constitutes the 'good life'. Nietzsche argues that this concept must be rethought in terms of his own reflections upon force, will and affirmation. The book also contains Nietzsche's most lucid introduction to the difficult notion of 'eternal recurrence', which assumes considerable importance in his subsequent work.

[1885] (1969) *Thus Spoke Zarathustra*, trans. R. J. Hollingdale, Harmondsworth: Penguin.

This is one of Nietzsche's most enigmatic books. It deals with his much-misunderstood idea of the 'Overman', which is the subject of Chapter 6. Nietzsche's adoption in *Zarathustra* of the narrative form of poetic fable, rather than the juxtaposition of philosophical aphorisms, lends it a vivid immediacy that many readers find attractive. Consequently, it is often recommended as a good point of introduction to Nietzsche's work. However, Zarathustra's teaching draws upon several of Nietzsche's key ideas that were set out at length in his earlier books. For this reason, the text's central contention – that a noble and aristocratic way of living is still possible for those free spirits who affirm their will to power, embrace *amor fati* and the eternal recurrence, and challenge the nihilism of contemporary morality – is better approached in the context of his earlier work.

[1886] (1990a) *Beyond Good and Evil: Prelude to a Philosophy of the Future*, trans R. J. Hollingdale, Harmondsworth: Penguin.

One of Nietzsche's most influential works, and one of the most famous philosophical texts of all time. Many readers might want to begin here in order to get a sense of what makes Nietzsche's work so challenging, disturbing, and hostile to conventional philosophical and moral assumptions. However, *Beyond Good and Evil* is a text to which one returns again and again because it contains passages that are absolutely central to his thought. Of particular interest here are the sections 'On the Prejudices of Philosophers', 'Free Spirits', 'On the Natural History of Morals' and 'What is Noble?' In these sections Nietzsche examines the rise and demise of strong and creative cultures, the will to truth and the history of moral values, and argues for an aristocratic mode of life beyond the moral categories of good and evil. A fascinating and absorbing book.

[1887] (2000) *On the Genealogy of Morality: A Polemic*, trans. Carol Diethe, Cambridge: Cambridge University Press.

Along with *Beyond Good and Evil*, this is perhaps Nietzsche's most important and influential book. It unquestionably represents his most significant contribution to political and ethical theory. Although the material is challenging, it is presented in an essay format that provides the space for the central concepts to be developed and explicated. The *Genealogy* consists of three essays that examine the historical evolution of such fundamental ideas as 'good', 'evil', 'justice', 'law', 'responsibility' and 'conscience'. It also presents Nietzsche's most extended discussion of master and slave morality, *ressentiment* and the will to truth. These essays offer a penetrating and powerful critique of our conception of morality, and constitute an indispensable element of an understanding of Nietzsche's work.

[1889/1894] (1990b) *Twilight of the Idols/The Antichrist*, trans. R. J. Hollingdale, Harmondsworth: Penguin.

Along with *Beyond Good and Evil*, these texts provide an excellent introduction to Nietzsche's work. Here, in condensed form, Nietzsche gives us an impassioned assault on some of the prevailing ideas of his time. In a hundred pages, *Twilight* presents a synopsis of Nietzsche's views upon the problem of morality, his critique of language and free will, his revelation of the real causality of 'metaphysical' ideas, his sense of his own relation to key thinkers in the western intellectual tradition, and much more besides. *The Antichrist* represents Nietzsche's most sustained attack upon institutional Christianity as an ascetic and life-denying expression of *ressentiment* and slave morality. It may profitably be read as a companion-piece to the first and third essays of *On the Genealogy of Morality*, where these themes are discussed in some detail. Both *Twilight* and *The Antichrist* offer excellent and highly readable examples of the wit and bite of Nietzsche's polemical style.

[Unpublished in Nietzsche's lifetime] (1992) *Ecce Homo*, trans. R. J. Hollingdale, Harmondsworth: Penguin.

Ecce Homo was written in 1888 during the last sane weeks of Nietzsche's life and published posthumously in 1908. The book constitutes Nietzsche's idiosyncratic autobiography. It is a fascinating and highly readable text, which restates a number of the main themes of his work. Nietzsche lays particular emphasis upon three themes: the status of his work as a tragic philosophy; the epochal importance of his revaluation of all values; and the ultimate triumph of Dionysius over Christianity and metaphysics that his work represents. Because Nietzsche adopts the titles of his major works for chapter headings in *Ecce Homo*, many casual readers assume that his remarks here crystallise everything that he thought valuable in these texts. This assumption should be resisted. *Ecce Homo* offers a highly selective, although consistently fascinating, account of his career, and there are signs that his mental state was impaired during its composition. Nietzsche's autobiography yields many startling insights, but their proper function is to point us back to the major works to which they refer.

[Unpublished in Nietzsche's lifetime] (1968) *The Will To Power*, trans. Walter Kaufmann and R. J. Hollingdale, New York: Vintage.

A collection of posthumously published notes containing fascinating insights into Nietzsche's views upon the nihilism of European culture, his critique of moral and metaphysical values, his theory of the will to power as the foundational movement of life, and his aristocratic vision of the relation between strong and weak modes of being. Because the integrity of these notes remains a matter of fierce scholarly dispute, the fact that Nietzsche never saw them through the press must always be kept in mind. A first version of *The Will to Power* was published by Elizabeth Nietzsche in 1900; a massively expanded edition was subsequently issued in 1906.

WORKS ON NIETZSCHE

Since the mid-twentieth century, a considerable number of books have been devoted to Nietzsche's work. The selection below includes some of the most useful places to begin reading about Nietzsche, and also highlights a few less introductory texts which have proved influential in the reception of his philosophy. The commentary provides brief details about the focus and level of complexity of the texts.

Allison, David (ed.) (1985) *The New Nietzsche*, Cambridge, Mass.: MIT Press.

An important, although quite demanding, collection of essays on Nietzsche by eminent thinkers such as Martin Heidegger, Jacques Derrida, Gilles Deleuze and Maurice Blanchot. These essays contributed considerably to a widespread revival of interest in Nietzsche by demonstrating how influential his work has been to contemporary European philosophy. They discuss key Nietzschean concepts such as the will to power, nihilism, the Overman and eternal recurrence. The collection assumes a good basic understanding of Nietzsche.

Ansell-Pearson, Keith (1994) *An Introduction to Nietzsche as a Political Thinker*, Cambridge: Cambridge University Press.

An excellent, clear and comprehensive guide to Nietzsche as a political thinker. Ansell-Pearson discusses Nietzsche's relation to both classical culture and modern political traditions in a lucid and accessible style that makes these issues available to readers relatively unacquainted with his work. The text also incorporates helpful reflections upon Nietzsche's style, and explicates key ideas such as genealogy and the Overman. An excellent starting point for discussion of Nietzsche's political philosophy.

Conway, Daniel W. (1997) *Nietzsche and the Political*, London: Routledge.

This is a clear and illuminating account of Nietzsche's political thought and his critique of modernity. Along with Ansell-Pearson, this text is the best introductory guide to the subject of Nietzsche's political philosophy. It situates his work within its proper historical context and provides useful readings of key passages in his texts.

Deleuze, Gilles (1983) [1962] *Nietzsche and Philosophy*, trans Hugh Tomlinson, London: Athlone.

This is a philosophically sophisticated and very demanding reading of Nietzsche as an anti-dialectical thinker of will, force and recurrence. Deleuze offers a startlingly original reading of key Nietzschean concepts such as genealogy, active and reactive forces, *ressentiment* and self-overcoming. Perhaps the most powerful reading of Nietzsche in recent years, it should only be attempted by the reader with a good knowledge of his texts.

De Man, Paul (1979) *Allegories of Reading: Figural Language in Rousseau, Nietzsche, Rilke and Proust*, New Haven: Yale University Press.

A highly complex, although very influential, reading of Nietzsche's rhetoric. De Man's deconstructive analysis explores the way Nietzsche's economy of metaphors produces, rather than merely describes, the idea of a 'pure' origin of concepts. This text assumes a knowledge of post-structuralist philosophy and is not aimed at the casual reader.

Derrida, Jacques (1979) *Spurs: Nietzsche's Styles*, trans. Barbara Harlow, Chicago: University of Chicago Press.

A complex deconstructive reading of Nietzsche's philosophical style(s) and the aesthetic character of his work. Derrida pays particular attention to the metaphorical quality of Nietzsche's philosophy and the will to power implicit in the rhetorical construction of different levels of being. This text assumes some background knowledge of Derrida's own philosophy in order to understand its main claims.

Foucault, Michel (1991) 'Nietzsche, Genealogy, History', trans. Donald F. Bouchard and Sherry Simon, in *The Foucault Reader: An Introduction to Foucault's Thought*, ed. Paul Rabinow, Harmondsworth: Penguin.

A fascinating and influential reading of Nietzsche's genealogical critique. Foucault was instrumental in reintroducing Nietzsche's work in the 1960s and 1970s. This essay examines Nietzsche's reflection upon force, will to power and perspective, and explores the implications of his rejection of teleological versions of history. Parts of Foucault's discussion are very demanding, but his essay also provides a very useful thematic analysis of one of Nietzsche's most elusive ideas.

Hollingdale, R. J. (1965) *Nietzsche: The Man and His Philosophy*, London: Routledge and Kegan Paul.

A very clear and illuminating critical biography of Nietzsche that provides a clear chronological and thematic introduction to his work. A very good point of departure for the casual reader.

Irigaray, Luce (1991) *Marine Lover of Friedrich Nietzsche*, trans. G. C. Gill, New York: Columbia University Press.

A highly sophisticated exploration from a feminist perspective of Nietzsche's use and repression of metaphors of fluidity.

Kaufmann, Walter (1974) *Nietzsche: Philosopher, Psychologist, Antichrist*, Princeton, NJ: Princeton University Press.

This book helped to rehabilitate Nietzsche's philosophical reputation in the 1950s after years of neglect. Kaufmann provides a comprehensive account of the thematic development and systematicity of Nietzsche's philosophy. Each of Nietzsche's main ideas is explained and their place within his system of thought clarified. The book also provides excellent exegetical readings of individual passages. It remains one of the few indispensable volumes for both the new and committed reader of Nietzsche. A classic.

Kofman, Sarah (1993) [1978] *Nietzsche and Metaphor*, London: Athlone.

A formidable deconstructive reading of Nietzsche's philosophical style, that pays close attention both to his exploration of metaphor and the system of metaphors employed in his own writing. This is by no means an introductory text, but it rewards close attention and is particularly useful for those readers interested in Nietzsche's style and use of language.

Magnus, Bernd and Kathleen M. Higgins (eds) (1996) *The Cambridge Companion to Nietzsche*, Cambridge: Cambridge University Press.

An excellent wide-ranging collection of critical essays on Nietzche's philosophy. The volume offers a broad introduction to Nietzsche's life and times, the thematic organisation of his work, his place within nineteenth-century philosophy and his influence upon modern and postmodern styles of thought. A very good starting point for the reader seeking a reliable general introduction to the issues raised by Nietzsche's work.

Megill, Allan (1985) *Prophets of Extremity: Nietzsche, Heidegger, Foucault, Derrida*, Berkeley: University of California Press.

This is an original and stimulating account of the challenge of Nietzsche's thought exemplified by his rejection of both a 'natural' and a religious morality and his emphasis upon the world and the human as aesthetically self-constituting entities. Nietzsche's influence upon modernity and postmodernity is elucidated in the context of the thought of Martin Heidegger, Michel Foucault and Jacques Derrida. This is a sophisticated, rather than an introductory text, which offers many insights into the relationship between Nietzsche and modern thought.

Nehamas, Alexander (1985) *Nietzsche: Life as Literature*, Cambridge, Mass.: Harvard University Press.

This is a clear, original and perceptive account of Nietzsche's work which manages to combine a broad thematic approach with philosophical rigour and close attention to textual detail. The ambitious reader might well start here, because Nehamas isolates and explains key constituents of Nietzsche's philosophy and supports his reading with a wealth of close analysis. For those readers who prefer to begin with a more explicitly introductory guide, Nehamas's book represents one of the necessary next steps to a full understanding of Nietzsche. The book is distinguished by a particularly clear and fine account of Nietzsche's perspectivism, aestheticism and the 'literary' character of his work on style and value. An excellent book.

Patton, Paul (ed.) (1993) *Nietzsche, Feminism and Political Theory*, London: Routledge.

An important collection of essays exploring feminist engagements with Nietzsche's philosophy. It presents illuminating rereadings of Nietzsche's critique of nihilism, *ressentiment*, reason, will to power and language. The text is just beyond introductory level, but the clear thematic organisation of the essays makes them rewarding for the reader with a reasonable grasp of Nietzsche's basic ideas.

Young, Julian (1992) *Nietzsche's Philosophy of Art*, Cambridge: Cambridge University Press.

A brief and lucid account of the development of Nietzsche's philosophy of art and its importance to his views upon metaphysics, ethics and politics. The level is well suited to the needs of the reader with some understanding of Nietzsche, and the book's clear focus upon the aesthetic enables Young to make many illuminating connections between different Nietzschean texts.

WORKS CITED

For bibliographic information on works by Nietzsche, see the 'Works on Nietzsche' in Further Reading section.

Adkins, A. W. H (1960) *Merit and Responsibility: A Study in Greek Values*, Oxford: Clarendon Press.

Blake, William (1989) *William Blake: The Complete Poems*, London: Longman.

Byron, George Gordon (1970) *Poetical Works*, Oxford: Oxford University Press.

Camus, Albert (2000) *The Outsider*, trans. Joseph Laredo, Harmondsworth: Penguin.

Coleridge, Samuel Taylor (1963) *Coleridge's Poems*, London: J. Dent & Sons.

Conrad, Joseph (1989) *Heart of Darkness*, Harmondsworth: Penguin.

Davis, Lennard J. (1997) *Factual Fictions: The Origins of the English Novel*, Philadelphia: University of Pennsylvania Press.

Deleuze, Gilles (1994) *Difference and Repetition*, trans. Paul Patton, New York: Columbia University Press.

Deleuze, Gilles and Felix Guattari (1984) *Anti-Oedipus: Capitalism and Schizophrenia*, trans. Robert Hurley, Mark Seem and Helen R. Lane, London: Athlone.

Derrida, Jacques (1978) *Writing and Difference*, trans. Alan Bass, London: Routledge.

Eliot, George (1994) *Middlemarch*, Harmondsworth: Penguin.

Eliot, T. S (1951) *Selected Essays*, London: Faber.

—— (1977) *The Complete Poems and Plays of T. S. Eliot*, London: Faber.

Foucault, Michel (1991) *The Foucault Reader*, ed. Paul Rabinow, Harmondsworth: Penguin.

—— (1992) *The Order of Things: An Archaeology of the Human Sciences*, London: Routledge.

Greenblatt, Stephen (1992) *Learning to Curse: Essays in Early Modern Culture*, London: Routledge.

Hunter, J. Paul (1990) *Before Novels*, New York: Norton.

Lawrence, D. H. (1985) *Three Novellas*, Harmondsworth: Penguin.

Lycos, Kimon (1987) *Plato on Justice and Power: Reading Book I of Plato's Republic*, New York: State University of New York Press.

Mann, Thomas (1971) *Death in Venice*, trans. H. T. Lowe-Porter, Harmondsworth: Penguin.

Miller, Arthur (1967) *Collected Plays*, London: Secker and Warburg.

Sartre, Jean-Paul (1957) *Being and Nothingness: An Essay on Phenomenological Ontology*, London : Methuen.

Shakespeare, William (1997) *The Norton Shakespeare*, ed. Stephen Greenblatt, London: Norton and Co.

Shelley, Percy Bysshe (1977) *Selected Poems of Percy Bysshe Shelley*, London: J. M. Dent & Sons.

Sophocles (1986) *The Theban Plays*, trans. Don Taylor, London: Methuen.

Stallybrass, Peter and Allon White (1986) *The Poetics and Politics of Transgression*, Ithaca, NY: Cornell University Press.

Stevens, Wallace (1984) *The Collected Poems of Wallace Stevens*, London: Faber.

Watt, Ian (1957) *The Rise of the Novel: Studies in Defoe, Richardson and Fielding*, London: Pimlico.

Winckelmann, Johann (1850) *The History of Ancient Art among the Greeks*, London: J. Chapman.

Woolf, Virginia (1984) *To the Lighthouse*, London: Panther.

Yeats, W. B. (1975) *Selected Poetry*, London: Pan.

INDEX

gods, Olympian 24
goodness 65–6
grammar 134
great politics 86, 110–14
Greeks 14; art 78; culture 23; self-annihilation 24
Groundhog Day (Ramis) 130–2
guilt 6

Harvard system ix
health, ill 3
Heart of Darkness (Conrad) 121
Hegel, G.W.F. (1770–1831) 30
Heidegger, M. 172
Henry V (Olivier) 71
herd instinct 96, 112
heritage, classical cultural 78
historians: moral ideas 96
historicism, new 158
history: antiquarian 82; critical 81; German 3; monumental 82; rethinking 157–8; uses 75–8
Hobbes, T. (1588–1679) 83
human: life 134; universal nature 8
Human, All Too Human (Nietzsche) 63, 95, 165
humanism 116–17
Hume, D. (1711–76) 66
humility 6

ideas, platonic 40
ideology: Nazi 86; notion 160
ill health 3
illusion, music and 25–8
imperialism, colonial 7
incest 19
individual, altruistic 91
individualism 145
industrial working class 3
injustice 97
interpretations 143
Intoxicated Song (Zarathustra) 128

intoxication: paroxysms 21
Introduction to Nietzsche, An (Ansell-Pearson) 169

Jews 101; *see also* anti-Semitism
Joyce, J. (1882–1941) 83
judgement: false 42; truth 42
justice 69, 76, 98, 99, 167

Kubla Khan (Coleridge) 33–4
Kurtz 121–3

Ladybird, The (Lawrence) 156
Laius 18
language 47, 135; deconstructive approach 159; German 46; two metaphors 47
law 69, 76, 167; absolute 48
legal system 99
liberalism 7
life 137; aim 137; hierarchy of force 139; human 134
Life of Friedrich Nietzsche, The (Förster-Nietzsche) 154
linguistic meaning 47
Lycos, K. 23
lying 46
lyric 25

Macbeth (Shakespeare) 61
man: creation of moral 62–5; higher 86; internalisation 70; sovereign 64; 'theoretical' 31–5; virtuous 29
mankind: self-transformation 123
Marine Lover of Friedrich Nietzsche (Irigaray) 171
Marriage of Heaven and Hell, The (Blake) 107–8
Mars 108
Marzrevolution (1848) 3
masculinity 161